SOCIAL AND ECONOMIC CHANGE IN EASTERN UKRAINE

Social and Economic Change in Eastern Ukraine

The example of Zaporizhzhya

HANS VAN ZON
ANDRE BATAKO
ANNA KRESLAVSKA
School of Social and International Studies
University of Sunderland

Routledge
Taylor & Francis Group
LONDON AND NEW YORK

First published 1998 by Ashgate Publishing

Reissued 2018 by Routledge
2 Park Square, Milton Park, Abingdon, Oxon, OX14 4RN
52 Vanderbilt Avenue, New York, NY 10017

Routledge is an imprint of the Taylor & Francis Group, an informa business

A Library of Congress record exists under LC control number: 97077538

ISBN 13: 978-1-138-38621-1 (hbk)
ISBN 13: 978-1-138-38622-8 (pbk)
ISBN 13: 978-0-429-42691-9 (ebk)

Contents

Maps, figures, tables and boxes

Maps

Figures

Tables

Boxes

Acknowledgements

The idea for this book developed during field work of Hans van Zon in Zaporizhzhya, financed by the ACE programme of the Commission of the European Communities. No serious analysis of the recent transformation of Zaporizhzhya society and economy has been made. Furthermore, reliable data about Zaporozhye is scarce and in most cases not published. When the three authors worked at the University of Sunderland on this book, they relied very much on the help of others, in and outside Zaporozhye.

Here we would like to thank more in particular Michael Brown, Jesper Lintholt, David Long, Ted Long, Raisa Usachova, Zaporizhzhya Statistical Office and the librarians of the University of Zaporizhzhya.

Introduction

Zaporizhzhya constitutes a typical example of an important industrial centre within the former Soviet Union. In the 1930s the attention of the whole Soviet Union focused on this new town. A huge dam and hydroelectric power station were build in the river Dnepr as well as Zaporozhstal, a gigantic steel enterprise. Many workers, from different cultural backgrounds, from all republics of the former Soviet Union, came to this town in Eastern Ukraine to build a bright future. At the same time Stalinist repression disciplined the population. Social engineering of the Communist Party had a deep impact on the new worker's town, with shallow cultural traditions. More than elsewhere, the population of Zaporizhzhya became passive and docile.

With the independence of Ukraine (December 1991) and the economic crisis associated with the dissolution of the Soviet Union and the collapse of centrally planned economy, the position of Zaporizhzhya changed fundamentally. From one of the major industrial centres in the former Soviet Union, producing electricity, steel, aluminium, cars, transformers and machinery, it transformed into a peripheral declining region in the wider European space, as a part of a new state that found itself in the margin of European politics. Transition towards a new economic system and insertion into the world economy changed many of the characteristics of Zaporizhzhya that once were considered as assets into obstacles. For example, the Soviet economy has been characterised by emphasis upon heavy industry and a high share of production for the military. For Zaporizhzhya these characteristics were even more pronounced. Nowadays, this legacy has become a barrier for change.

Moreover, Zaporizhzhya, located in Eastern Ukraine and not far from Russia, has suffered a lot from the dissolution of the Soviet Union. As a result of all these changes Zaporizhzhya has faced unprecedented industrial decline: more than 60 per cent during 1991-1997.

In Zaporizhzhya province about 2 million people have lived through a major drama. This drama is reflected in dry figures: in 1996 no European country had as low a birth rate and as high a mortality rate as Zaporizhzhya province had. The result is that the population of Zaporizhzhya is declining rapidly. The desperation of the population is reflected in one of the highest suicide rates in Europe and extremely high levels of alcohol abuse. More than half the population of Zaporizhzhya town is de facto unemployed. At the same time, a small group enriches itself on a massive scale.

It is noticeable that there are hardly any publications about the drama undergone by the population of Zaporizhzhya in recent years. This is related to the lack of openness in Zaporizhzhya society. This book can be seen as a contribution to the needed debate about ongoing social and economic change. The book not only builds upon the scarce, mostly unpublished sources available about Zaporizhzhya but also upon personal experiences of the authors. Two of the three authors lived for a long time in Zaporizhzhya.

The book focuses on the most important changes that occurred recently in the province of Zaporizhzhya, especially since the independence of Ukraine (1991).

A short account of the history of Zaporizhzhya shows how history, including pre-Revolutionary history, is still very much visible in present day Zaporizhzhya (Chapter 1). Independence for Ukraine has meant a major historical rupture as suddenly Zaporizhzhya changed its orientation from Moscow to Kyiv, the new capital. It also meant the Ukrainisation of Zaporizhzhya town, that is in majority Russian speaking. This process not only implied the marginalisation of the Russian language, but also of culture as well. (Chapter 4).

Chapters 2 and 3 describe the emerging economic and political system as the development of a kleptocracy, tolerated by a passive population, in which many elements of the Soviet and Tsarist past are discernible. The redistributive syndrome, in which funds are channelled towards loss-giving state-owned enterprises while squeezing profitable enterprises and the population at large, prevents economic development.

Prospects are gloomy for the eight large industrial enterprises that constitute the base of industrial Zaporizhzhya. These enterprises, that work with obsolete outlays, are hardly restructured (Chapter 5).

The increasing divide between the countryside and towns is dealt with in Chapter 6. The deepening agricultural crisis is rooted in the economic system that de-motivates agricultural producers to work.

The financial crisis of the state caused the rapid decline and crisis of a range of public services: health care, education, public housing, public transport, etc. A social and material infrastructure, built up during decades, broke down in a few years. The breakdown of this culture and care for pensioners and disabled is analysed in Chapter 7. Chapter 8, dealing with social change, describes the atomisation of society and the developing crisis of gender relations, spreading poverty as well as crime.

Chapter 9 describes how Zaporizhzhya province became one of the most polluted regions in Europe: one out of every three hospital patients suffers from a disease caused by environmental pollution, especially from polluted drinking water. Declining production, and subsequent declining emission levels, did not prevent a rapid increase of diseases related to environmental pollution. The huge nuclear power station near Zaporizhzhya town, the largest in Europe, is a source of major concern to the population, due to its increasing level of malfunctioning.

Apart from environmental pollution and declining health care levels, it is also increased poverty levels that contribute to a health crisis. In particular, young children and middle-aged men suffer from all kind of diseases. An explosion of sexually transmitted diseases has struck the youth (Chapter 10).

Surprisingly with all the above described changes, Zaporizhzhya society remained to a high degree closed and inward looking. Internationalisation remained largely confined to the bazaar. Zaporizhzhya became one of the major export regions of Ukraine, exports being mainly semi finished products, like steel and aluminium. On the other hand, foreign direct investment is at a very low level. Zaporizhzhya markets were flooded with Western products, while Ukrainian products were not competitive.

The book shows how developments in various spheres are interrelated. It describes the mechanisms of underdevelopment. An important element here is the typical socio-psychological syndrome (Appendix 1), consisting of a set of attitudes and behavioural routines, with deep historic roots, that helps to reproduce a stagnating socio-economic system. Apparently, a social base for modern economic development is not yet existent in present-day Zaporizhzhya.

1 The Making of Modern Zaporizhzhya

Alexandrovsk

Zaporizhzhya is built on the wide steppe plains of South-eastern Ukraine, on both sides on the river Dnepr, about 500 km from Kyiv, the capital city. Until 1921, Zaporizhzhya was a small town called Alexandrovsk and located in Ekaterinaslav.

Up to the late 18th century no sedentary agriculture could develop in these borderlands of the Russian empire because they were regularly swept by invasions of nomadic tribes from the East. These borderlands in the steppe of South-eastern Ukraine were then named Zaporizhzhya, which means 'beyond the rocks' (in the Dnepr). Up to that time the region had been a stronghold of the Cossack warriors who are credited with defending Russia and Ukraine against the Tartars and Turks.[1] According to the historian Seton Watson, among the Cossacks were

> many fugitive serfs, fleeing from their Polish landlords. In the area around the rapids of the Dnepr a considerable military power was established by the Zaporizhzhya Sich, a Cossack community with a primitive social and political organisation of their own, who recognised no other law, and conducted warfare and diplomatic manoeuvres between Poland, Muscovy and Crimea.[2]

In 1707 - 1708 there was a major conflict between the Cossacks. Under the leadership of Mazepa, ataman of Ukrainian Cossacks and based in what is nowadays Zaporizhzhya, this movement got control over a larger part of Southern Russia. Peter I crushed this revolt with great cruelty.

The Cossacks found, among others, a refuge on the island of Hortitsa, located in the Dnepr in present-day Zaporizhzhya.[3]

Tsarina Catherine II annexed the Crimea in 1783, subduing Tartar tribes that had prevented the development of sedentary agriculture in Southern Ukraine and who kept Ukraine largely depopulated and insecure. From that time onwards the vast steppes of Southern Ukraine were converted into arable tillage and planted by a stable, sedentary peasant population living on large estates.[4] Catherine started, and Tsar Paul continued, a policy of colonisation by foreigners, especially Germans. Under Catherine 75,000 foreigners came to Little Russia, having been given four million acres and advanced nearly six million roubles, of which one-third was a gift.[5]

Socially, this clearance of arable land subjugated the once free or semi-free inhabitants to the conditions of the central peasantry, which meant serfdom. Agricultural technology was very primitive. More than half of the peasants had wooden ploughs. Yields were very low. The aristocracy was generally not interested in agricultural management. However, some forward-looking landlords introduced machinery.[6] Despite the backwardness of agricultural technology, in Ekaterinaslav province 80 per cent of land was for export crops. South-eastern Ukraine became the bread basket of the Empire.

During the nineteenth century, a backward socio-economic system, based on serfdom, developed in the countryside of what is now Zaporizhzhya province.[7] Although in 1861 serfdom had been abolished and the former serfs could, in principle, buy the land that they cultivated, a labyrinth of traditional forms of extra-economic surplus extraction, embodied in customary rights and dues, continued to prevail on estates in what is now Zaporizhzhya province. Peasants paid the landlords with part of the crop and provided the landlord with various services.

Probably related to the recent nature of its submission, the peasantry was more prone to revolt compared to the peasantry in the heartland of Russia. In the revolutionary upheavals at the end of World War I, the Ukrainian anarchist Makhno, who controlled a considerable part of Ukraine in 1921, had his base in Zaporizhzhya province.[8]

South-eastern Ukraine was one of the more backward regions of the Russian empire. In 1887, 13.6 per cent of the inhabitants of Ukraine were literate (women 3.9 per cent), compared to 29.3 per cent for the Russian empire as a whole (women 13 per cent). This is partly related to the fact that education was in the Russian language.

South-eastern Ukraine was early this century still overwhelmingly agrarian. People were mainly occupied in farming. Handicrafts and trade were poorly developed. Social and economic development was hampered by feudal relations. From the mid-19th century onwards, the absolutist state was the major engine of rapid industrialisation from above. However, this touched the region of what now constitutes Zaporizhzhya only to a very limited extent.

In Tsarist times, the role of the state was overwhelming. The nature of state was absolutist. Even priests of the Orthodox Church were considered as state functionaries. The state furthered the system of anonymous letters accusing fellow citizens and according to which citizens could be convicted. The higher ranks in the extended state bureaucracy were hereditary and linked to the nobility. The state, the landlord class and bureaucracy formed a single unity. The state had integrated feudal hierarchy into the bureaucracy.[9] Corruption was widespread.[10] In the womb of this feudalism, embryonic capitalist relations developed from the mid-19th century onwards.

Alexandrovsk was created in 1770 around a fortress. The town became an administrative centre for the immediate neighbourhood. In the 19th century, a railway was built that passed through Alexandrovsk. Until the October revolution in 1917, Alexandrovsk was a quiet town. Only a very small minority, mainly Russians and Jews, lived in the towns.

The area of what later became Zaporizhzhya province suffered much during World War I. In 1921, during the civil war, there was a major famine. There were many conflicts in this region due to its strategic nature. South-eastern Ukraine, with its dense concentration of industry, communications and agricultural potential, was of vital importance for Russia. The Bolsheviks were very weak in what is now Zaporizhzhya province.[11]

The emergence of modern Zaporizhzhya

Under Soviet rule, Alexandrovsk, later renamed Zaporizhzhya, became known as a symbol of Soviet power. The electrification of the country was seen as a main goal of the Soviet government. According to Lenin, socialism meant Soviet power plus the electrification of the whole country. A huge dam and hydroelectric power station were built on the Dnepr at Zaporizhzhya in 1932 to further this goal.[12] Soviet literature describes the heroic efforts of the inhabitants of Zaporizhzhya to create the impressive industrial complex and the dam. People from all over the country came to Zaporizhzhya to build a new future. In the eyes of many, the will of masses of mobilised people accomplished a miracle. For many it seemed that a big step in the direction of a bright future had been made. For many all over the Soviet Union, the building of the dam and the building of Zaporozhstal

Ukraine

Zaporizhzhya province

meant that the Soviet people could build the best of all worlds. The people of Zaporizhzhya were proud and nowadays, many families have relics that remind them of those heroic times.

Less is known about the hardships people had to undergo. For example, for a long time a larger part of the population had to live under primitive circumstances in barracks.

In the period of pre-war five-year plans, Zaporizhzhya developed into an important industrial centre of the Soviet Union with 63,000 industrial workers. People came from all corners of the Soviet Union, mainly from the countryside. They were mostly poorly educated workers with a peasant background, attracted by the comparatively high wages they could earn in Zaporizhzhya. However, in many cases they were also attracted by the challenge of contributing to a new socialist future.

Generally, South-eastern Ukraine witnessed a rapid development in those years, compared with the rest of Ukraine. The gravity point of industrialisation within Ukraine moved towards the South-east. Especially in the Donetsk basin, east of Zaporizhzhya, many new towns arose. The population of Zaporizhzhya increased from 50,000 inhabitants in 1926 to 275,000 inhabitants in 1939 (425,000 inhabitants in 1959).

Large steel factories, an aluminium plant and a magnesium-titanium plant were built in Zaporizhzhya during the 1930s. The new industrial complex allowed the Soviet Union to become less dependent upon deliveries from the capitalist world. By 1937, Zaporizhzhya was supplying 60 per cent of aluminium produced in the Soviet Union, 100 per cent of manganese and 20 per cent of steel plates.[13]

During the 1920s and 1930s huge efforts were made to eradicate illiteracy, with great success.

During the 1930s a collectivisation campaign, in which private farmers were forced to join collective farms, ravaged the countryside. In the Ukraine, approximately 2.5 million persons died in the famine (1932-1933) that was provoked by the forced confiscation of all grain reserves. Stalin ordered the expropriation of all foodstuffs in the hands of the rural population. The odd thing was that enough food was available and grain was being exported to the West. The province of Zaporizhzhya objected to the imposed quotas for grain delivery. The local party committee told both the Ukrainian central committee and its own district committees that 70-75 per cent of the quota would have to come from poor and middle-income peasants; and this might leave them without sufficient seed and would not leave 'a single kilogram' of grain for sale to the local population.[14] Most victims were in the southern belt, in which also Zaporizhzhya province is located.[15]

However, the famine struck Zaporizhzhya less hard than Dnipropetrovsk. On the borderlands between Dnipropetrovsk and Zaporizhzhya the army prevented starving people from seeking refuge in Zaporizhzhya province. Many died as a consequence of repression and famine. As a result, the population of Ukraine declined between 1926 and 1939 by 10 per cent.[16] Many farmers were deported to Siberia.

The world of heroic efforts to build modern Zaporizhzhya and the world of repression and famine seemed to be two completely different worlds.

During World War II, major battles were fought in and around Zaporizhzhya which was largely destroyed in these battles. During World War II all industries were evacuated to the far east of the Soviet Union. For example, equipment from Zaporozhstal was used to build steel factories in Magnitogorsk and Novosibirsk. 'Motor Sitch', producing aircraft engines, was evacuated to Omsk where in three months time production started. To prevent its usefulness to the Germans, Soviet demolition squads destroyed part of the dam across the Dnepr during 1941. In 1943 the Germans shelled and bombed it as they fell back, destroying what remained of the factories. More than 400 factories in the province, 21 of national significance, lay in ruins.

Zaporizhzhya city itself was a wasteland in which 300,000 war-weary, desperately hungry and exhausted people sought to make homes in dugouts, squalid huts and the crumbling shells of what had been apartment houses. No large buildings had survived the war.

The war with Germany has forged a new unity of the people, grouped around the aim to get rid of the invader. Repression was somewhat relaxed and the Orthodox Church rehabilitated by the state. The victory over Germany gave the space for a new big mobilisation campaign to rebuild destroyed Zaporizhzhya.[17] Leonid Ilyich Brezhnev was appointed as the first secretary of the provincial party committee. In order to rebuild Zaporizhzhya the best workers were selected from the whole of the former Soviet Union. More than 13,500 people helped to rebuild the hydro-electrical power station and 20,000 workers rebuilt Zaporozhstal. Zaporozhstal started production again in 1947.

After the victory over Nazi Germany, hardships were not over for the population. Stalinist repression again struck hard and illusions were crushed anew. For example, shortly after the war, the secret service took out of every third house one or more people and shot or deported them to Siberia. This arbitrary repression was meant to terrify and discipline the population. Terror was particular severe in Zaporizhzhya. Everyone felt the fear as anyone could become a victim of Stalinist repression. Anonymous letters could send people to death camps. A woman in Zaporizhzhya threatened to accuse a man of disloyalty to the Soviet state unless he married her as she was pregnant. Nevertheless she sent after the marriage a letter to the secret service with the result that he died in a concentration camp. Everybody knew the story of Pavel Morozov who became a hero after he betrayed his parents, accusing them of anti-Sovietism. It was the fear related to this repression that had a lasting impact upon the mentality of Zaporizhzhya citizens.

The party leadership traditionally has seen Zaporizhzhya as a kind of human laboratory. Regularly policy measures were tested in Zaporizhzhya before carried out elsewhere. Social engineering was easier in a new town like Zaporizhzhya. It had also to do with the fact that the eyes of the whole Soviet Union were directed on Zaporizhzhya. National party newspapers reported regularly about the rebuilding of Zaporizhzhya. Again, Zaporizhzhya became a showcase. The town was also an example for the creation of the new Soviet man. People from the whole of the Soviet Union came to the melting pot of Zaporizhzhya that was being moulded into a typical Soviet town, in which Russian emerged as the major language. It became a typical worker's town with shallow cultural traditions. The second wave of immigration also brought many released prisoners, which helped to shape the cultural traditions of Zaporizhzhya.

For a long time, people had to live in bad circumstances. Many lived in barracks, without toilets, usually without hot water and sometimes without cold water as well. At the same time, Zaporizhzhya became known as an example of Soviet town planning. Characteristic is, compared to other Soviet type towns, the greening of the residential districts. As is typical for all Soviet towns, various urban functions are not segregated but mixed, very polluting industrial districts are located close to the centre of town, that is alongside Lenin Avenue. This avenue is about 12 kilometres in length. Major social and cultural centres are located around this axis, which means that Zaporizhzhya does not have a real town centre. Remarkable for Zaporizhzhya, compared to Western towns of similar size, is its provincial nature. Anywhere in town, and even immediately around Lenin Avenue, one can find quiet courts and parks. Zaporizhzhya looks like a provincial town with a low level of social and cultural services. There is no historical centre, although on the eastern side of town some historical buildings remained intact. Many historical buildings were destroyed during the war or broken down as a result of long-term neglect. Nowadays, the few remaining historical buildings are in decay, such as the Lishenski house, in front of the theatre. The communist secret service ordered the destruction of all churches.[18]

After World War II, the industrial complex was reconstructed and expanded. A transformer factory added in 1949, a factory producing electrical machinery in 1951, a titanium-magnesium plant in 1956, a car factory in 1959 and a factory producing aircraft engines. In the 1960s big electromechanical enterprises were being constructed including Zaparozhkabel and Preobrazovatel. The industrial complex profited from vast deposits of minerals in the region and from the neighbouring regions; minerals included coal, iron ore, manganese ore and titanium. In the mid-1980s Zaporizhzhya produced nearly half of all the stainless and ball-bearing steel in the Soviet Union, a third of cold rolled steel and about half of transformers for electricity generation.

Zaporizhzhya developed into a town of 897,000 inhabitants (1992), while Zaporizhzhya province totalled 2,077,800 inhabitants (1995). This latter figure means that exactly 4 per cent of the entire Ukrainian population lives in Zaporizhzhya province.

The disintegration of socialism in Zaporizhzhya

The socialist world has witnessed a process of relative gradual decline and disintegration since the mid-1970s. With the revolution in microelectronics and communications going on in the Western world, it gradually became apparent to the ruling elite in the socialist countries that the socialist world has lost the economic and military competition with the West. It was obvious that the so-called socialist world market (COMECON) could not provide an alternative for the capitalist world market. Up to the early 1980s it was mainly leading scientists who hinted in Eastern publications at this phenomenon. During the 1980s politicians, mainly from the reform-minded countries also spoke about it. There was a process of economic stagnation and growing awareness among the ruling elite in the socialist world that problems of modern economic development could not be solved anymore in the context of a centrally planned economy of the Soviet type. Although the governments tried to conceal this crisis by trying to protect the population to a certain extent from the consequences of this stagnation - by investing less and borrowing from the West - the population in most countries noticed economic stagnation by declining living standards and growing scarcities.

Extensive economic growth (more of the same) could be realised in the context of the Soviet-type planned economy. However, this economy could not bring about intensive economic growth, i.e. growth through innovation and continuous restructuring of the economy.

Typical for Zaporizhzhya was that this developing crisis of socialism went largely unnoticed by the ruling elite and population of Zaporizhzhya. Up to the mid-1980s life in Zaporizhzhya was quiet and living standards continued to improve gradually. There were no dissidents. When Gorbachev came to power and began to speak about the mounting crisis, many people in Zaporizhzhya were surprised to hear about such a development. Zaporizhzhya was to a large extent shielded from the political changes described above.

Under party leader Brezhnev political leaders in the regions had more scope of manoeuvre to solve regional and local problems, on the condition, however, of strict loyalty towards the centre. In contradistinction to Soviet rule under Stalin, under Brezhnev political leaders at all levels felt more certainty about their positions. They were less threatened by sudden displacements or dismissals. This relative stability for bureaucratic and political functions had the consequence of an ossification of power and of the emergence of a gerontocracy. In political and bureaucratic careers, seniority became more important. Also in Zaporizhzhya a process of feudalisation of political power occurred. For example, the clique around party leader Vsevolozhki, who reigned in Zaporizhzhya for about 15 years, acquired more and more privileges. Jobs were distributed among family and friends.

Due to the greater stability of political and bureaucratic careers, and also the gradual 'liberalisation' for leaders at the local and regional level, more scope for corruption arose. Up to the 1960s, probably a majority of the population believed in socialism and this belief could provide a motor for development, despite repression. Gradually, since then, more people became disillusioned and began to see the negative sides of social development. Although with the death of Stalin people did not have to fear for their lives any more, repression became more refined. Everyone has been supervised by the state in many ways. An extended network of informers of the secret service made sure that nobody could openly express his or her opinion. When one of the authors of this book complained on the steps of the university building about the quality of education, she was called one day later by the rector and asked for an explanation for her criticism. Another author of this book listened one evening to the BBC in his student room, whilst alone. One day later the pro-rector reproached him for listening to anti-Soviet radio stations.

Everybody had to reckon with the fact that approximately one out of three adult citizens worked with the secret service. Especially during the sixties and seventies the system of anonymous letters spread. The party felt obliged to research accusations of each anonymous letter.

As time passed, fewer people could believe the propaganda of the party-state. Although people tolerated power through their passivity, active party support dwindled as the illusions that inspired many people up to the early sixties gradually disappeared.

Important changes came with the coming to power of party leader Mikhail Gorbachev (1985). Glasnost and perestroika were introduced. However, in the early years, this did not have much positive impact upon the political climate in Zaporizhzhya. The local press did not become more liberal and the local ruling elite continued to rule in the old way. One could find in Zaporizhzhya a kind of 'socialism' that had disappeared long ago in Moscow and St Petersburg. In 1989 *Pravda* criticised the party leadership in Zaporizhzhya for its conservatism.[19] Nevertheless, the population gained more scope for self-organisation and a number of new social organisations developed. In the late 1980s the role of the intelligentsia became more pronounced in the political sphere and many had the hope that something could change. During the late 1980s reports were made public in which all kind of problems in Zaporizhzhya society were openly discussed. The reports about environmental pollution and related health problems were especially shocking (see Chapter 9). For the national parliamentary elections independent candidates were brought forward and the reform minded journalist Vitali Tchelishev managed to get a seat in the Soviet parliament. His critical column in *Industrialnoje Zaporizhzhya* became famous.

However, it seemed that the world outlook of most people did not change. Therefore, the collapse of communism and the dissolution of the Soviet Union in 1991 came as a big surprise for most people. Few had expected the collapse of the mighty party-state axis that had dominated society for such a long time. People could not judge the depth of the developing crisis of socialism as they had nothing to compare it with.

The process of disintegration became also visible in Zaporizhzhya. The problem of scarcities became more urgent starting in 1985, when Mikhail Gorbachev came to power.

Party leader Gorbachev gave more scope for private activities in the framework of the 'co-operative movement'. However, given the bureaucratic context in which these co-operatives had to develop and the gradual criminalisation of power as well as the growing scarcities, the emergence of co-operatives was linked for many with the criminalisation of the economy.

Due to growing scarcities, many big enterprises in Zaporizhzhya began to extend their systems of services for their employees: they began to buy kolkhozes, install meat factories etc. A divide appeared between those workers working for big enterprises with an extended service sector, and those workers who were dependent upon the normal and badly functioning state service infrastructure.

Although under Gorbachev enterprises gained more autonomy, at the same time the percentage of national income redistributed through the state budget continued to rise.[20] Also, the share of heavy industry in national production continued to increase, at the expense of consumer goods production. Wages of workers rose during the 1980s, especially since 1985, but the provision of consumer goods lagged behind. This caused inflation and gave greater scope for black marketeers. The failure of official distribution channels spawned a proliferation of black markets, corruption and economic crime under Gorbachev. Living standards in Zaporizhzhya began to decline.[21] Gradually, hope in a better future began to vanish.

Hence, although the Gorbachev reforms have been widely applauded in the West as a big step towards democracy and the market economy, in Zaporizhzhya many negative accompanying features were more prominent. Glasnost had in Zaporizhzhya less consequences as the party leadership did not change and followed docilely the conservative party leadership in Kyiv. Only in the period 1989 - 1992 was the local press allowed to be somewhat critical. The political activities of representatives of the local intelligentsia slowed down in the early 1990s and disillusionment spread. The thaw in Zaporizhzhya politics was very short.

Thus, the Gorbachev era has meant in Zaporizhzhya primarily an accentuation of the traditional deficiencies of socialism. It meant the open disintegration of socialism that would subsequently lead to the collapse of the party state, central planning and the demise of the Soviet Union.

Notes

1. Some authors, like Y. Bystrysky, speak about the heroic myth of Zaporozh Cossacks as contributing to the new Ukrainian identity. Cossacks ('free men') were mostly peasants, who fled southwards between the 14th and 18th century from economic and political oppression, and from serfdom. They set up autonomous communities, ruled by an elected leader (ataman). Sometimes they served the Russian state, sometimes they fought it. All special Cossack institutions were abolished by 1920 by the Bolsheviks.
2. Seton-Watson (p. 7). According to Malet (xx) 'Sich' was a 'byword for absolute self government, living off plunder, mainly at the expense of the Turkish communities of the Crimea and the northern Black Sea coast.'
3. It was also on this island that from the late 18th century onwards German Mennonites settled. Nowadays descendants of these German settlers still live in Zaporizhzhya. Regularly, foreign Mennonites visit Zaporizhzhya to learn about the history of these German settlers.
4. Perry Anderson considers this agrarian colonisation of Ukraine as probably the largest single geographical clearance in the history of European feudal agriculture.
5. Malet, p. xviii.
6. Berdyansk became the site of the largest manufacturer of threshing machines in the Empire and one of the largest in Europe (Malet, ibid.).
7. 'The incredible figure of 99.9 per cent of serfs were on barschina, under which they were obliged to work the land , as of old, and not allowed to commute this service for money (obrok). By contrast, in the central districts, only 41 per cent of serfs were on compulsory field work.' (Malet, p. xviii)
8. Makhno, a Ukrainian school teacher from Gulai Pole, in what is now Zaporizhzhya province, led a peasant guerrilla that fought against the forces of Danilov and Wrangel (the anti-Bolshevik, 'White' forces), but gradually he refused to co-operate with the Red Army. From Gulai Pole he raided Ekaterinaslav province. He even briefly took the province capital, a sizeable city, and he tried to put anarchistic theory into practice. At times, his army counted several thousands of soldiers, armed with weapons taken from the enemy. Nowadays, Ukrainian nationalists make a national hero out of Makhno.
9. The word 'feudal' should be used with due caution with respect to Tsarist Russia. See Chapter 3.
10. In a memorandum, P.A.Valuyev who served as a provincial governor under Nicholas, wrote in 1855: 'The variety of administrative forms outweighs the essence of administrative activity, and ensures the prevalence of the universal official lie. Glitter at the top, rot at the bottom. In the creations of our official verbosity there is no room for truth. It is hidden between the lines, but who among official readers is always able to pay attention to the space between the lines?'(Seton-Watson, p. 210).

---

11. The Soviets were in the hands of Social Revolutionaries and Makhnovists. As late as 25 November (8 December, Russian calendar) the Mensheviks and Social Revolutionaries still had a majority in the Soviet of Alexandrovsk, the Bolsheviks having 95 seats of 232 (Malet, p. 5).
12. Most of the equipment for this dam was supplied by General Electric. American engineers helped in constructing the dam (Dornberg., pp. 74, 94).
13. *Ocherki Istorii Zaporizhzhya*, p. 50.
14. 6 October 1929, as quoted in Davies, p. 71.
15. The three foremost experts on the famine wrote together an article in which they came to the estimate of 2.5 million victims. Only in 1988 did historians in the Soviet Union began to write about the famine (see interview with the historians S. Kul'chytskyi, R. Solchanyk).
16. Conquest, p. 22.
17. German prisoners rebuilt part of the town in the period 1943 - 1949. Also slave labour has been used to rebuild Zaporizhzhya.
18. Churches were destroyed in the Soviet Union according to a systematic plan. Destruction took place by town in alphabetical order. Therefore Zaporizhzhya was one of the first towns where this destruction began. Because Kharkiv is at the end of the cyrillic alphabet, many churches in Kharkiv were spared.
19. See *Wall Street Journal*, 21 November 1989.
20. The percentage of utilised national income redistributed through the state budget increased from 53.3 per cent in 1970 to 73.5 per cent in 1989. (Koropeckyi, p. 33).
21. See G.E. Schroeder, in Koropeckyi, p. 280.

2 The New Economic System

Transition in Ukraine

In Ukraine, and therefore also in Zaporizhzhya, transition towards market economy started later than in most other Central and East European countries. Gorbachev came to power in 1985 and started a campaign for glasnost (openness) and perestroika (reconstruction). However, Ukraine has, to a certain extent, been shielded from these changes due to the conservative party leadership. Shcherbytskyi, a Brezhnev crony, stayed in power from May 1972 till September 1989.[1] In 1991 independence came as a gift, through the falling apart of the Soviet Union. This dissolution, combined with the change of the economic system, has lead to a steep decline in production.

The decline has been steeper than in most other post-socialist countries. Whereas in the countries of Central and Eastern Europe (excluding the former Soviet Union) real GDP in 1996 was 88 per cent of the level of 1989, this percentage was 54 per cent for the Community of Independent States and 42 per cent for Ukraine.[2]

Transition in Ukraine is not only characterised by the fact that it started later than in most other post-socialist countries, but also because it is proceeding slower. Communism was more deeply rooted here compared to many other regions of Eastern Europe and therefore the preparedness for change was less.[3] This is reflected in the low level of public support for reforms. Due to the long-standing isolation of the Ukraine, knowledge of market economy is minimal. Generally, the competence of the Ukrainian governing elite is rather low. This is a significant difference from Moscow, where a large fund of knowledge about how to govern a country has been accumulated.

The Ukrainian economy is performing worse than Russia's.[4] This is connected with a number of factors. Ukraine is a major energy importer, unlike Russia. Before the dissolution of the Soviet Union, Ukraine paid only 3 per cent of the world market price for oil, while it is now on the world market level. In 1996, imports of fuels and fuel derivatives accounted for 52 per cent of total Ukrainian imports.

Box 2.1 The economic structure of Zaporizhzhya

The economic structure of Zaporizhzhya is typical for industrial regions based on heavy industry the same situation could be found in Western Europe and the USA in their early phases of industrialisation.

Thirty-four per cent of the working population was employed in industry, 16 per cent in agriculture, 9.7 per cent in education, 8 per cent in construction, 6.5 per cent in transport and communication and 7 per cent in health care in 1994. Within industry, in 1995 55 per cent was employed in machine building and metal processing, 16 per cent in heavy metallurgy and 7 per cent in electroenergy.

The economy of the province is dominated by 360 large enterprises, especially eight very large ones. The role of small and medium-sized enterprises is modest, although rapidly growing. The latter enterprises are mainly in trade and services sectors. By early 1996, there were 7000 active, private tax-paying enterprises, mostly small and medium-sized.

The economic structure is distorted in the sense of a hypertrophy towards industry, especially heavy industry, and the heavy weight of big enterprises. Many enterprises are monopolists in their branch. There is a very low share of finished products in total industrial production. Very few consumer goods are produced in Zaporizhzhya province. About 70 per cent of the machine building industry used to produce for the military. Examples are Motor Sitch, producing engines for jet fighters, Iskra and Radiopribor. Another component is the developed energy industry. On the one hand there are the hydroelectric power stations, on the other hand there is a nuclear power station. There are a lot of energy-intensive industries in the province. The Titanium Manganese Enterprise, Aluminium Enterprise, Ferrosplavzavod and Dneprospetsstal consume together 80 per cent of all produced electrical energy in the province.

Most of the industrial enterprises in Zaporizhzhya have outdated equipment, in many cases dating from the 1930s.

Industry in Zaporizhzhya is export-oriented. Twenty-one per cent of total production was exported in 1995. This is a very high share compared to the national average. Zaporizhzhya accounted for 8.5 per cent of the total exports of Ukraine in 1995. Zaporizhzhya, together with the three neighbouring regions of Donetsk, Luhansk and Dnipropetrovsk, account for more than half of total Ukrainian exports.

This all means that the energy shock has been enormous.An additional difficulty lies in the fact that Ukraine is a new state. Unlike Russia, in Ukraine the demarcation of competencies between president, government and parliament has not yet been settled.

Another characteristic of transition in Ukraine is the fact that the shadow economy has acquired an enormous dimension and accounts now for approximately 60 per cent of estimated Gross Domestic Product.[5] In the countries of the former Soviet Union this share is estimated at, on average, about 40 per cent, in the Latin American countries at about 30 per cent.[6] Therefore it has become very difficult for government to implement an economic policy. The postponement of the privatisation of state-owned enterprises contributed to the growth of the shadow economy. Experts from the Ukrainian Centre for Social and Economic Research think that in Ukraine the shadow economy constitutes 'not only a shadow sector in the economy but a parallel illegal power, that grows and begins to duplicate the most important functions of the state'.[7]

Related to this problem is that of lawlessness in the economy. Contracts have a very limited value in Ukraine. This increases transaction costs in the economy enormously, and has kept away many potential foreign investors.

The government has contributed greatly to the growth of the black economy through the high level of taxation. The mechanism is as follows: the government is confronted with a budget crisis, partly related to subsidies to loss-giving enterprises, and tries, increasingly, to reduce the deficit by cutting expenditures and raising taxes. As a result enterprises try to evade taxes and move to the black market. As more economic activities move into the shadow economy, the burden on the legal, registered and non-subsidised part of the economy becomes heavier, to the extent that legal economic activities by companies are rendered very difficult. The Ukrainian government has, up to now, not found a way out of this vicious circle.

In the shadow economy organised crime increasingly imposes its rule. According to a report written for President Kuchma, organised crime now poses an immediate threat for the stability of the state. The criminal subculture has penetrated all levels of the state apparatus. Organised crime has its parallel power structure and the population has to pay for these structures (see Chapter 8). On average, organised crime makes products 20 to 30 per cent more expensive. Few firms can escape organised crime: about 90 per cent of firms are under its influence.[8]

A large share of exports and imports are illegal and capital flight has acquired enormous proportions.[9] Income disparities seem to have increased more than in other Central European countries. Impoverishment of a large share of the population is beyond levels attained in the greater part of the rest of Central and Eastern Europe. Liberalisation of prices occurred in a situation in which in many branches enterprises were monopolists. This contributed to hyper-inflation that has been brought under control since mid-1995.

Ukraine also has to pay a high price for the Chernobyl disaster. This fact is little known in the West.[10] In addition, Ukraine has a disproportionally high ageing population.[11]

This list of characteristics of Ukrainian's transition to market economy leads to the conclusion that in Ukraine this transition has been one of the most cumbersome in Europe, not taking into account the countries that suffer under the devastating effects of war. This description of Ukraine as a whole also applies to Zaporizhzhya.

Industrial decline in Zaporizhzhya

Recent data of the Zaporizhzhya Statistical Office show that industrial decline in Zaporizhzhya province did not start until 1992, with a very steep decline in 1994. According to the Zaporizhzhya Statistical Office, in 1991 growth of industrial production was 0.4 per cent. In 1992 the decline in industrial production was 4.7 per cent, in 1993 1.2 per cent, in 1994 22.5 per cent, in 1995 10.3 per cent and in 1996 industrial production increased by 0.4 per cent. On the basis of earlier data of the very same statistical office it can be argued that annual industrial decline was higher by about 3 - 4 per cent (see Appendix 2). On the basis of circumstantial evidence, real decline in industrial production must have been even higher (see Appendix 2).

Important to note here is that, according to Zaporizhzhya statistical office, steep industrial decline begins in 1994. This is much later than in most other regions and countries of Central and Eastern Europe. This fact contributes to an understanding of the lack of preparedness of the elite of Zaporizhzhya for market-oriented reforms.

The level of agricultural production in Zaporizhzhya was in 1995, 60 per cent of the level of 1990.[12] The decline in this sector has been larger in Zaporizhzhya then in the Ukraine as a whole.

Many will try to argue that the decline in production is less dramatic, by taking into account the rapid increase of the shadow economy, that is not reflected in official statistics. This sector accounts now for about 60 per cent of the estimated Gross Domestic Product (GDP). According to a report, written for President Kuchma, if the weight and growth of the shadow economy are taken into account, the decline of GDP between 1989 and 1994 may be in the range of 25 per cent. On the other hand, statistical figures point at the rapid spread of poverty and misery and indicate a steep falling of living standards of the vast majority of the population that is far beyond a drop of one quarter of real income (see Chapter 8) An assessment of the fall of GDP with inclusion of the shadow economy came to an estimated drop in GDP between 1990 and 1995 of 31.7 per cent.[13]

The falling apart of the Soviet Union has especially affected Zaporizhzhya; located close to the Russian border, its supply and demand systems are very dependent upon Russia and other republics of the former Soviet Union. While 56 per cent of all industrial enterprises in Ukraine were under the all-Union ministries, in the Donetsk-Dnepr region (Donetsk, Luhansk, Dnipropetrovsk and Zaporizhzhya) it was 69 per cent and in Zaporizhzhya province even 72 per cent.[14] In the case of Zaporizhzhya, more outputs and more inputs come from outside the region than would have been the case for a region with a similar economic structure in the developed West.

By mid-1997, the economy was still dominated by very large enterprises that are *de facto* state owned, although formal privatised. Market economy hardly existed, although enterprises were faced with harder budget constraints and had better insight into real production costs. Big enterprises still function in an economy that is redistributive, i.e. the state still subsidises and keeps many enterprises afloat. This redistributive economy is in crisis and operating in a context that is increasingly constrained by world market forces.

Although the provincial administration boasts with figures that indicate that 7.5 per cent of all privatised firms in the Ukraine are in the province (population 4 per cent), these figures should be interpreted with great caution. Fewer shops are privatised in Zaporizhzhya compared to other big towns and only in 1995 was the first private hotel opened. It is in the sphere of services that, usually, in post-socialist countries, the first wave of privatisation takes place.

In 1995, the privatisation of industrial enterprises began, and by mid-1997, this privatisation process was still in its early phase. Motor Sitch, the aircraft engine producer in Zaporizhzhya, was one of the first big enterprises to be privatised, and immediately a big scandal arose because the privatisation agency suddenly withdrew an additional 17 per cent plus 27 per cent of the shares from the auction, with the result that most of the shares will remain state owned. The argument was that the enterprise was of 'strategic importance' for Ukraine, an excuse frequently used to avoid privatisation.[15] Gradually it appears that with the corporatisation of enterprises, in many enterprises the state will get hold of the majority of shares.

Although the privatisation processes proceeded very slowly, managers of state-owned enterprises succeeded in appropriating state-owned property and making illegal profits through selling abroad. In 1993 there were still large inventories in the enterprises. Using these low- or no-cost materials, the enterprises still could sell a lot of products abroad for another two or three years, for low prices. Real costs were usually not taken into account. As reserves dwindled and enterprises were forced to taken into account higher energy prices and higher prices of new inputs, prices became, in most cases, non-competitive.

In 1996 and 1997, the large enterprises were in a process of corporatisation. The commercialisation process is still in its initial phase. Big enterprises have numerous possibilities to get state support by tax exemptions and cheap credits. Marketisation is also hampered by the wide-spread practice of corruption and the absence of a law-governed economy. Laws simply do not function. Breaking of the law has in principle no consequence. This gives vast opportunities to corruption and organised crime. Business can not operate without dealing with organised crime and corruption which has become a way of life.

The development of the economy is hampered by prohibitive taxation. High inflation[16] and the underdeveloped banking system make industrial development extremely difficult.

The large state enterprises have hardly adjusted to the new circumstances. Organisational changes seldom occurred. Few have been fired. Although the official unemployment figure is 0.15 per cent (1995), *de facto* unemployment, in the form of unpaid leave, amounts to more than half of the working population.[17]

Does Zaporizhzhya has a regional economy?

Enterprises in Zaporizhzhya hardly functioned in the context of a regional economy. In Soviet times, most enterprises worked under the supervision of the branch ministries in Moscow that organised all inputs and distributed all outputs. These ministries did not take into account a rational utilisation of productive forces in a spatial context and neglected the advantages of intra-industry trade. It often happened that some inputs came from the far east of the Soviet Union, while the very same inputs could have been provided by an enterprise in Zaporizhzhya, but that happened to be subordinated to another ministry.

Transformerzavod imported in 1991, 22.3 thousand tonnes of steel, 4.8 thousand tonnes of copper and 5.7 thousand tonnes of aluminium from Russia and 27.2 thousand tonnes of copper from Uzbekistan. Note, and this is typical, that also large quantities of inputs have been imported, like steel and aluminium, that are also produced in Zaporizhzhya.[18] Avtozaz imported 22.5 tonnes of steel from Russia, while there are huge steel factories in Zaporizhzhya. Melitopol motor factory imported 676 tonnes of steel and 392 tonnes of rolled steel from Russia.[19] The picture arises of a region that was highly integrated into the Soviet economy, but with a limited regional coherence. However, the regional economy has been designed as a coherent complex, centred on the hydro-electrical power station and given the local natural resources. The question comes here to the fore as to what extent a more rational spatial pattern of supply chains has developed after the collapse of communism.

With respect to output, similar data as for inputs are not available, but it is known that most large enterprises produced for the Soviet market as a whole and many of these enterprises even were monopolists. For example, Avtozaz was the only producer of cheap cars for the entire Soviet Union. Motor Sitch, which was incorporated in the military industrial complex, delivered to the aviation industry located elsewhere in the former Soviet Union. Eighty per cent of engines for Soviet military transport aeroplanes were made in Zaporizhzhya.

With the falling apart of the Soviet Union many links with the republics of the Community of Independent States were severed and contributed to a large degree to the economic decline of Zaporizhzhya. Many links are still there as is reflected in the geographical composition of export and imports, but at a much lower level then in 1991. Another problem is that with the falling away of former links, few new links within the region have been established.[20]

With the dissolution of the Soviet Union the Ukraine tried to restore vertical connections with enterprises formerly resorting under the control of ministries in Moscow through its own industrial ministry in Kyiv. This policy was a complete failure. At the same time, the social consequences of this policy had to be solved by the local and regional authorities.

In January 1993, there was an order from the president to give more power to the regions. But this order did not change anything. Gradually a situation developed in which the regions began to govern themselves *de facto*, doing this however without a legal base. *De jure*, the ministries governed.

With a manifesto of 10 points for the development of a regional policy, the (former) provincial administration of Zaporizhzhya went in 1992 to neighbouring provinces. A coordinating committee had been formed by the provinces of Donetsk, Dnipropetrovsk, Luhansk and Zaporizhzhya. One result of this initiative was that coal was organised for the electricity generating stations. Another result has been that 26 November 1993, Kravchuk, the president of the Ukraine, gave Dnipropetrovsk, Donetsk, Zaporizhzhya and Luansk substantially more scope for self-governing. However, a problem remained that of unclear competences of regional administration and national ministries. Therefore many initiatives have been blocked.

Nowadays, Zaporizhzhya provincial administration does not have more scope of manoeuvre than other provinces. The opportunity, given at the end of 1993, has not yet been taken. The years 1992 - 1993 constituted a short interlude of increased autonomy for the regions. Since then the central administration again gained more powers. Nowadays, the overwhelming part of state funds, i.e. 82 per cent, is distributed by national government.[21]

The provincial administration of Zaporizhzhya also asked a Western consultant firm, after an open tender, to make a regional development plan for Zaporizhzhya.[22] In 1993, the firm Coopers and Lybrand delivered such a plan, the first for a region in the former Soviet Union.[23] However, practically nothing has been done with the recommendations given in the report.

Nowadays, Zaporizhzhya provincial administration has not developed a genuine regional policy, although a good regional policy seems urgent in view of the economic and social crisis. Nowadays, the approach to regional problems is more of an *ad hoc* nature, trying, like a fireman, to run from one fire to another not taking the time to get an overall view. Significantly, no research in the regional economy has been done, and attempts at such research are even hampered by the provincial administration. The approach towards regional problems has been rather of an administrative-command nature than facilitative. The newly established Regional Development Agency has not played any role in the development of a regional policy.

An interesting initiative has been the agreement of cooperation between neigbouring provinces in Ukraine and Russia, in which Zaporizhzhya also is participating (27 January 1995). It appears that on this level cooperation is easier than on the level of governments. Nevertheless, since its inception, nothing has been heard of this initiative.

Small and medium-sized industrial enterprises

A big change in the economy of Zaporizhzhya has been the emergence of a large number of small and medium-sized enterprises, most privately owned. Very few are active in industry. Most of these industrial enterprises have grown out of state-owned enterprises.

With high interest rates, high taxes and declining demand, it is especially difficult for small and medium-sized industrial enterprises to develop. They are particularly sensitive to the bad debts problem and lack of credit.

In particular small and medium-sized enterprises are vulnerable to Mafia influence. Without bribing local administration officials it is practically impossible to survive. The former Ukrainian vice-minister of economy, Viktor Pyznyk, estimates that in order to open a small business in Ukraine, you need to hand out nearly 2000 dollars in bribes.[24] This all means that entry costs are rather high. According to many business people interviewed in Zaporizhzhya, the number of small and medium-sized enterprises declined since 1994 as purchasing power of the population diminished rapidly and as the local bureaucracy created numerous obstacles to private entrepreneurs, especially those producing goods.

Financial infrastructure

High-level inflation is one of the main obstacles for industrial development. High inflation makes medium and long-term credits unattainable for industrial enterprises. Therefore banks are lending mostly to trading firms.[25]

Inflation and bad debt chains have led to a partial demonetarization of the economy. Many enterprises ask payment on delivery and even then problems may arise. Most enterprises have to operate with barter deals, often with the help of middlemen. Often, employees get paid in kind, that is, with the products their factory produces. They then have to spend much time to sell these products. For example, it happened that an employee of a construction enterprise went to the bank with a lorry load of sugar that he has got as salary, asking for money. As the sugar was very cheap, the employees of the bank bought the sugar. The enamel factory pays its employees in pans. Enterprises have to spend much energy in organising barter deals, in order to secure supplies. The pump factory in Berdyansk (Zaporizhzhya province) conducted 90 per cent of its trade (including supplies) in barter. Out of 3000 employees 120 were involved in the organisation of barter deals. Another example: the textile factory Vepes (Zaporizhzhya) produces overalls. Ninety per cent of its deliveries are paid for with products. For instance, Vepes gets steel for the delivered overalls. Subsequently the steel is exchanged for spare parts with a factory in Nikopol (Zaporizhzhyia). These parts are exchanged for black steel with Zaporozhstal. Then this steel goes to the barrel factory in exchange for paint. This paint goes to Transformerzavod that gives cash money.

Unwillingness to deliver may lead to disruption of a whole supply chain. For example, in July 1995, 50 - 70 per cent of the workers of Avtozaz were send on unpaid leave because the motor factory in Melitopol could only deliver one-third of the ordered parts. The reason for this was that they could not get a spare part from a factory in Luhansk that wanted payment in advance. However, the factory in Melitopol did not have enough cash to meet the request.[26]

Banks are developing rapidly and the level of services is improving although still at a very low level compared to Western countries. However, opening an account still costs at least 10 dollars for personal accounts and about 100 dollars for enterprises. A Visa card can only be used since early 1996, at one place in Zaporizhzhya, for a tariff of 4.5 per cent. Only in September 1996 was the first Ukrainian Visa card issued.[27] In 1995 the first wall cash machine in Zaporizhzhya appeared at Avtozaz bank. Usually, bank services are extremely expensive and service is bad. Often, interest rates are fixed on a individual basis. In mid-1997, interest rates on loans were up to 20 per cent a month.

Dealing in cash is difficult if not impossible. Banks are mainly used for transfers between enterprises. Wages are usually paid in cash. Enterprises can only have a very small part of money in cash. They are obliged by the state to do most transfers, except wages, by bank. It are especially industrial enterprises that find it difficult to circumvent this rule.

In Zaporizhzhya many banks developed out of state-owned enterprises or as a means to whitewash illegally obtained money, for example, the foundation of the Avtozaz bank. Formerly Avtozaz used the services of the national bank. At a given moment the Avtozaz directors thought it would be profitable to found its own bank. The management of the Avtozaz bank took 3 months of the employees salaries to provide the starting capital for the bank. After some time a state controlled commission discovered that the starting capital was not enough. Shares were sold, in particular to higher management levels. In this way higher management became the *de facto* owner of the bank. Other big enterprise banks were established in a similar manner.

It is usually family clans that control banks and it is very difficult for competent outsiders to get jobs.

What new economic system is emerging in Zaporizhzhya?

In mid-1997, Zaporizhzhya was still in the very early stage of transition to a market economy. The economy can be characterised as redistributive in a monetary non-transparent way. Public authorities still do not know exactly what activities are subsidised or not. They subsidise, apart from health care and education, a large share of the housing costs of the population and a large share of public transport. On another level, that of national government, many enterprises are kept afloat by subsidy. On top of this, more than half of all economic activities are in the black market sphere and therefore not paying taxes. As a result an increasingly smaller share of the economy, the sound enterprises, have to support an increasingly larger part of the economy. This burden has become unbearable and the economic base of this redistributive economy is eroding quickly. Policy makers apparently are not aware of this mechanism and continue to subsidise loss-giving economic activities with the argument of preserving the social balance. In this way the Gordian knot of the redistributive economy becomes even tighter.

As the purchasing power of the population declines further, the state has to pay a greater share of subsidised activities. By mid-1997, in Zaporizhzhya about half of tenants could no longer pay for rent, heating, water and telephone. At the same time the state has decided that tenants should pay about 60 per cent of expenditures for apartments. Public transport and other public utilities are faced with less income. Subsequently, the financial crisis of the state is aggravated, exerting greater pressure to enhance taxes. As a result of the financial crisis, local authorities decided to reduce sharply the delivery of warm water and the heating of apartments has been reduced.

So the vicious downward spiral perpetuated. The politicians are very busy discussing the redistribution of the declining economic cake, instead of discussing the introduction of new economic mechanisms that may enlarge the cake.

In other post-socialist countries similar mechanisms have arisen. However, the peculiarity of the Ukraine in general, and of Zaporizhzhya in particular, is that destructive forces are predominating over constructive forces. Zaporizhzhya is far from the point where the market economy has attained a critical mass.

It is difficult to characterise the emerging economic system in Zaporizhzhya because the present economic system is still very fluid and unstable. Also, by mid-1997, there were scattered islands of different economic structures that functioned under different economic laws. For example, the state-dominated big enterprises function in a totally different context compared to the small and medium-sized private enterprises. The major part of the population that survives by retreating to more primitive forms of economic activity functions in another economic environment than the newly established banks. Nevertheless, there are common features in the economic environment of all those fragments of the economy of Zaporizhzhya. There are also major trends discernible. If identifying major driving forces and major actors and factors in the present configuration of social, political and economic forces, it is possible to sketch the most likely scenarios of economic development.

One major factor is the bureaucracy. Although there is a verbal commitment to market economy, the present economy and society are still to a large extent bureaucratised. It can be considered as a kind of tumour that is not easily removed. Public authorities are programmed to think in terms of controlling people and enterprises. There is a control mania in society that suffocates all independent economic activities. This mania cannot be abolished by central government simply decreeing the changeover to a market economy. So, the bureaucratic control mania seems to be a structural factor in social and economic life of Zaporizhzhya.

People and enterprises can only survive by designing strategies to circumvent bureaucratic control. They can do this by moving in the grey or black market sphere and by corruption. A bureaucratised society and corruption go more or less together. Government reacts to the black economy by trying to control and to tax even more. Thus there is a symbiosis between the large black market sector and bureaucracy. The same applies for organised crime that has infiltrated all segments of the economy. The spreading of crime is intricately linked with the control mania of bureaucracy. On top of that, society is administered by a ruling elite that is not at all interested in social and economic development. A lasting factor seems the criminalisation of the business class. Different criminal groups are competing to create 'protection' for enterprises.

All these structural factors in Zaporizhzhya society create a dynamics of underdevelopment that is characteristic for many less-developed countries.

Many will argue that Ukraine has the characteristics of a developed country, considering the high levels of education and industrialisation. However, education levels are only measured in terms of persons having finished higher education. Skills needed in a modern economy are often absent. More importantly, it seems that a set of deeply rooted attitudes hampers modern economic development (see Appendix 1). Nowadays, it appears that no social base for modern economic development exists in Zaporizhzhya.

Also, the industrialisation level is declining rapidly as Zaporizhzhya, and Ukraine at large faces a process of rapid de-industrialisation. This is historically a unique process. Never before has a region or country witnessed such a rapid de-industrialisation.

Many of the features that are often considered as features of modern economic development are in fact not. The economic system that is emerging is not geared towards enhancement of the production of goods, because the producer of wealth is immediately squeezed by both bureaucracy and criminal groupings. The criminalised economy is inherently unstable as it is not able to generate social and economic cohesion. The lack of social and economic cohesion is matched by an overdose of coercive power. People are disciplined by fear.

In the present unstable situation it is easier to get rich by stealing or trading, than by producing goods or services. The short-term perspective predominates in Zaporizhzhya. Many expect that if the economic situation stabilises, in terms of low inflation, less economic decline etc., automatically a situation will emerge in which it will become profitable to produce and to develop a long-term perspective. However, the lack of a law-governed economy is structural and this prevents the emergence of a modern economy.

It is not the market economy that has attained a critical mass, but instead a criminalised bureaucratically co-ordinated redistributive economy.

Conclusion

In Zaporizhzhya, and Ukraine at large, transition to a new economic system has been a much more cumbersome process than in most other regions of Central and Eastern Europe. A kleptocracy emerged, combined with the perseverance of a redistributive economy, channelling funds towards large loss-giving enterprises. The economy of Zaporizhzhya is still very much dominated by the state, in the context of the absence of the rule of law. The economy has only been to a limited extent liberalised.

The new economic system that is emerging, albeit still fluid, seems to generate a dynamic of under-development rather than the searched-for smoothly functioning, wealth-generating market economy.

Notes

1. Gorbachev did not undertake any purge of the Communist Party of the Ukraine to bring it more in line with Perestroika and Glasnost policies, probably due to the fear of creating centrifugal forces in the second largest republic of the Soviet Union.
2. Economic Commission for Europe, 1997, p. 225.
3. Slowdown of economic growth occurred in the Soviet Union later than in most Central and Eastern European countries. Slowdown of economic growth occurred in Ukraine later than in other Soviet republics.
4. Whereas the real wage in Ukraine was in 1992 9 per cent higher than that of Russia, in September 1996 the Ukrainian real wage was only 59 per cent of that of Russian real wage (*Economist Intelligence Unit*).
5. From the 1960s up to the late 1980s the shadow economy increased gradually in the Soviet Union (by a factor of 30 as is maintained in *Zerkalo Nedeli*, 10 February 1996) to attain about 20 per cent of gross domestic product in 1990. The largest shadow economy is found in agriculture, then in trade and construction and to a lesser extent in industry (see *Ekonomika Ukraini*, November 1996).
6. *Zerkalo Nedeli*, 10 February 1996, p. 5.
7. *Ekonomika Ukraini*, November 1996, p. 11.
8. *Zerkalo Nedeli*, 10 February 1996, p. 6.
9. A government agency estimated that in the period 1991 - 1995, $15 - 20 billion were illegally exported (*Zerkalo Nedeli*, 10 February 1996, p. 9). The

International Herald Tribune (10 April 1997) wrote that American and Ukrainian officials estimate that as much as $100 billion has been spirited out of the country by profiteering officials.

10. The Ukrainian government has introduced a special tax for combating the consequences of the Chernobyl disaster. In 1992 the share of Chernobyl funds available in the state budget was 15.7 per cent, in 1995 this percentage has dropped to 5.1 per cent (Greenpeace, 1996). For comparison: in 1995 1.9 per cent of state expenditures were for science.
11. In Ukraine, there are for one pensioner 1.5 working people, in Russia this rises to 1.8, in France and the United States to 2.5 and in Japan to 2.6 people.
12. Zaporizke, 1996b.
13. *Ekonomika Ukraini*, November 1996, p.14.
14. Koropeckyi, p. 127.
15. *Kyivskie Vedomosti*, 6 July 1995, p. 6.
16. According to the Ukrainian Statistical Office in 1992 inflation was 2,100 per cent, in 1993 10,256 per cent, in 1994 501·per cent, in 1995 281 per cent and during 1996 80 per cent. There is clearly a declining trend although present inflation rates still hamper very much economic development.
17. *Delovaya Ukraina*, 15 November 1995, p. 12. There are also many people that work and do not receive payment. Personnel of schools and health care institutions by the end of July had only received payment over February.
18. The explanation in this case is that the aluminium plates used for transformers were not and are not produced in Zaporizhzhya. The special steels, needed for transformers, could not be produced in Zaporizhzhya. Similar explanations can be find for the supply of steel for Avtozaz. Of course, the question can be posed why no provisions have been made so that these supplies could have been produced in Zaporizhzhya.
19. *Industrialnoje Zaporizhzhya*, 12 March 1991.
20. For example, Prof. R. Niethammer, who did research in Zaporizhzhya, pointed to the fact that a factory in Zaporizhzhya did not stock an indispensable screw that used to come from Russia. But he discovered that literally around the corner, 500 metres away, an enterprise could manufacture the same screws. Lack of contacts had prevented the factory from discovering this itself.
21. *Zerkalo Nedeli*, 10 February 1996, p. 7. Much more is distributed by the central state apparatus compared to other countries of comparable size.
22. Germans in Kyiv, with the support of the German embassy, have initiated this process. Germany, unlike many other Western states, was interested in regenerating industrial potential in Central and Eastern Europe. Zaporizhzhya represented an interesting case. Later came the support of the EU-TACIS programme.
23. Financed under the TACIS scheme for the amount of $700,000.

24. He estimates that managers spend over a third of their time dealing with rules and regulations. A survey found that it costs Ukrainian enterprises nearly $900 in bribes for a telephone installed and nearly $300 for an import licence (*Business Central Europe*, June 1997).
25. In early 1996, about 11 per cent of credits of the 200 most important banks in the Ukraine were long term. During the first half of 1996, 65 per cent of the money of Ukrainian banks were allocated in state bonds that guaranteed 100 per cent dividend (a high return compared to the 40 per cent interest rate of the National Bank of Ukraine), while industrial investments composed only 3 per cent of all investments (Egorov,I.)
26. *Novosti*, 14 July 1995, p. 3.
27. *Kyivskie Vedomosti*, 5 October 1996.

3 The Nature of Power

Town and provincial administration, as well as large enterprises and the most important social and economic institutions are still headed by people who used to govern in communist times. At first sight, for the general public, they seem to govern in the same way, in an authoritarian manner, in a sphere of secrecy, in the absence of the rule of law and not hindered by opposition or a critical press.

However, many elements in the way Zaporizhzhya is ruled have changed. In this chapter the focus will be on the relationship between continuity and change in the organisation and structure of power, the differentiation within the ruling elite, the meaning of parliamentary democracy in Zaporizhzhya, the role of the news media, the system of interest representation and the working of the bureaucracy.

Former communists still in power

The Communist Party in Zaporizhzhya had a huge apparatus that in Soviet times duplicated the state apparatus. It fulfilled an essential role in moving and controlling society and economy. Party officials were present in each enterprise, in each institution and every town district. What happened with this huge apparatus when the party-state collapsed? What happened with the fortunes the party controlled?

The Nomenklature that occupied state functions and stayed in power after the formal demise of communism created new jobs, mainly for party functionaries, in the local and provincial administration.[1] As a result, between 1990 and 1996 the number of officials in the municipal and provincial administration more than doubled.[2] Often, new departments were created in order to allow party functionaries to get a place. In most cases, these party functionaries stayed in the same office, only the name of the office changed.

This does not mean that nothing changed. The Communist Party stopped controlling every aspect of social and economic life and lost its function of facilitator in social life. The party disappeared as motivator of all kind of enterprises and institutions to do their work properly. The disappearance of this engine function created an integrational vacuum in society.

In big enterprises often new semi-independent departments were created in which party officials found their place. For example, in Dneprospetsstal a new department for foreign trade was created, later becoming independent, where former party functionaries got a job. Frequently it was commercial structures that succeeded in siphoning off profits and assets of enterprises. Leaders of Komsomol often succeeded in getting hold of new commercial structures, such as the conglomerate Hortitsa and the tourist office. The Nomenklature also appropriated party property by creating a lot of new enterprises. In such a way, the transformation of the party elite into a kleptocracy has been completed in several years.

On the other hand, the fact that the party-state collapsed did not mean that old organisational routines rooted in the party-state, disappeared. The collapse of the party-state can be compared with a dragon with multiple heads. Although the main head, the communist party-state axis, collapsed, the dragon continued to live with its minor heads. For example, after the fall of communism, in Avtozaz ritual meetings were regularly organised for its personnel with communist-style pep talks in which trade union leaders fulfilled their traditional role, now redefined as transmission belt for the enterprise leadership. Nowadays, the most important link for Avtozaz in Zaporizhzhya is no longer the party headquarters in Zaporizhzhya but the province administration, although many people there used to work for the party. They simply changed labels.

Has power in Zaporizhzhya a feudal character?

The former, vertically structured organisation of society and economy around the hierarchical party-state axis has been replaced by a complicated system of mutual horizontal dependencies, without a clear centre, but run by the same people.

The guiding principles of the functioning of the protection networks within the ruling elite hark back to classical European feudalism and Russian tsarism. Similarities to classical feudalism include the absence of the rule of law, the disregard of the interest of the masses and the rights of the individual, the neglect of social and economic development in general and the system of loyalties governing the relations between those in power.[3] Another major similarity with feudalism is the privatisation of political life.

Bureaucrats and politicians regard their institutions as their temporary private property.

A feudal trait is also to the system of clans and the loyalty of clans to supreme power. It echoes the complicated networks of seigneurs and vassals in feudal society. Feudal is the complicated system of loyalties that gives the ruling elite of Zaporizhzhya a certain cohesion. No one in a leading position is allowed to step out of line. For example, the local newspapers are dependent on gifts of local administration and big enterprises. Therefore, they can not afford to write critically about local society.

Similarities with Russian tsarism include the central place of the state bureaucracy in the power structure as well as the symbiosis and unity of various dominant social and economic interests around the state bureaucracy. But the character of state power changed from totalitarian, trying to control all aspects of the life of citizens, to authoritarian, trying to impose its rule by authoritarian means, without rule of law, but allowing some scope of manoeuvre for citizens as far as they do not threaten existing power arrangements. Whereas in late European classical feudalism particularist interests, centred around the bourgeoisie, the Catholic Church, the nobility and other groupings, forced the rulers to strive after regulations between these groups, a kind of social contract, nowadays in Zaporizhzhya, as in tsarist Russia, such particularism seems to be absent.

The feudal traits of Zaporizhzhya politics had already emerged in Soviet times. Brezhnev's rule gave politicians and bureaucrats more existential certainty by avoiding random dismissal and promoting the system of ancienity in bureaucratic promotions. Also, the need to delegate competencies to lower levels and the need to allow more scope for informal mechanisms in the economy contributed to a feudalisation of regional political cultures (see also Chapter 1).

Differentiation within the ruling elite

Whereas in communist times the party - state axis was the clearly recognisable centre of power, nowadays the power structure is much more opaque. It is a non-transparent system of protection lines, a system of various clans that more or less co-operate. The system of loyalties, based on mutual services and governed by tacit codes, is across political party lines. The web of loyalties has a high density around the key figures in the ruling elite, i.e. around the directors of the largest enterprises, the mayor, the province council, the head of the secret service and so on.

It is difficult to distinguish groupings within the ruling elite. There is on the one hand the corpus of red directors, i.e. the directors of large enterprises. There is the group of leading figures in the media landscape, the directors of academies and the directors of hospitals. They all belong to the leading stratum who know each other and who are directly dependent upon the political centre. The large enterprises wish to be included in the network of local interest groups because they may profit in many ways from hidden subsidies. Directors of state - funded organisations and institutions are usually appointed by the town or provincial administration and can be easily dismissed if they break the 'rules of the game'.

There is also the group consisting of representatives of new commercial structures, for example the new powerful banks and conglomerates like Hortitsa, an enterprise that founded its power on the selling of state property and that now has activities in many different spheres. The leaders of these new banks and large commercial enterprises are often from the former Komsomol, and usually somewhat younger than the 'old' Nomenklature in power. It is remarkable that there are no signs that the representatives of these new groupings threaten the cohesion of the ruling elite in Zaporizhzhya. A struggle for power is not visible.

Like the representatives of the old Nomenklature, these new economic groupings do not seem to be interested in economic development and do not have a long-term perspective.[4]

The ruling elite of Zaporizhzhya has its protection lines in Kyiv. From the viewpoint of Kyiv, power structures in Ukraine have a clear regional, i.e. territorial base.

In politics, as in public life in general, distrust reigns and only family and 'old boys' that one knows from youth and with whom one has developed a life- long close relationship can be trusted. That explains, for example, why President Kuchma has given a large number of key posts on the national level to trustees from Dnipropetrovsk. Brezhnev selected many of his old friends from Dnipropetrovsk and Zaporizhzhya to high posts in government. For example, V.E. Dymshits, from Zaporizhzhya, has become a deputy minister and A.P. Kirilenko became a member of the Politburo.[5] As in the Byzantine world of politics personal loyalty is of primordial importance, clans at the national level often have a territorial base, because old friends' cliques began their collective career in specific localities.

Selection mechanisms for influential posts in Zaporizhzhya society are such that the affiliation with specific clans, or the old Nomenklature in general, is more important than competence to do the job. In communist times it was loyalty to the party leadership nowadays loyalty towards the former communist bosses is required. These selection mechanisms are not challenged by democratic forces. Democracy conceived as a system of countervailing forces, in which the general interest may be reflected on the political level, is virtually non-existent in Zaporizhzhya.

The selection mechanisms within the ruling elite, and the absence of appointment mechanisms regulated by law, further the cohesion of this elite. Dissident behaviour can be punished immediately.

Parliamentary democracy and interest representation

Against the background of the mechanisms of the political process in Zaporizhzhya as described above, it becomes clear that parliamentary democracy is only a facade. Most people believe that elections in Zaporizhzhya are manipulated. It is also remarkable that with the municipal and provincial elections only slightly more than 50 per cent turned up to vote. Probably, the actual number of voters must have been less than 50 per cent.[6]

How is it possible that the electorate voted mainly for former members of the Nomenklature? To this end we have to explain the electoral system in which political parties do not play a role. Individuals may only be candidates in elections if they have gathered enough signatures among the population. Lobbies around enterprises organise support for specific candidates. Enterprises systematically approach their personnel telling them for whom to vote. The voters usually do not know the persons on the list themselves. Therefore, they usually vote for the recommended persons. The result is that the representative bodies in Zaporizhzhya are filled with members of the former Nomenklature. They are often associated with the Communist and Socialist parties.

The other parties are associated with the 'democrats' who are blamed by a large part of the population for all changes since the mid-1980s, although they have never been in power in Zaporizhzhya. Another factor that may explain voting behaviour is the patriarchal relationships between rulers and ruled. Most people do not see alternatives to the present power structure in Zaporizhzhya and blame all kind of hardships to external factors: Russia, the government in Kyiv etc. They are inclined to follow the 'advice' of their leaders. They are docile.

Democrats are usually so disappointed with politics in general that they often abstain from voting. In a certain sense, the electorate in Zaporizhzhya does not want to be an electorate. Thus, the popular vote sanctioned the traditional power structure and contributed to the fact that in many respects Zaporizhzhya remained a communist society.

It is important to note that parliamentary democracy in Zaporizhzhya, and in Ukraine at large, was not a demand of the people, as in most parliamentary democracies. The changes were decreed by the government. The result is that there is little or no grassroots demand for change. The people by their docile nature, learned under Soviet rule, are slow to complain and demand reform. The lack of an active media contributes to the passiveness. It is for these reasons, apart from the fact that the overwhelming part of the economy is still in state hands, that the present phase of transition can be considered as the last phase of communism rather than the first phase of the establishment of modern parliamentary democracy. The legacy of communism is still overwhelming while parliamentary democracy is still in an embryonic phase.

Disintegration of the old system is prevalent and the set of attitudes developed under Tsarism and communism, like passivity and compliance, still very much hampers social and economic development (see Appendix 1).

Political parties are not parties in the Western sense as they do not compete for voters with alternative electoral programmes. Having asked the local liberal party, with a membership of several dozens, for a programme, they could only give a national programme in which vague goals are described.

The main political parties in Zaporizhzhya province are the Ukrainian Republican Party (3,900 members), the Communist Party (3,700 members), the Labour Party (2,800 members), the Liberal Party (1,100 members) and the Agricultural Party (900 members) (as of 1997).

Politics in the Western sense, where opposing views and interests are expressed publicly in the context of a quest for power, is not existent. Politics is not seen in the context of alternative options. Those in power seem to see their task as the administration of society. Politicians are bureaucrats in Zaporizhzhya. Politicians and bureaucrats operate in secrecy. This attitude is rooted in the absolutist tradition of the administration of society.

Interest-representing organisations like trade unions hardly fulfil their role as they still are mainly linked to the ruling circles. Entrepreneurs are better organised, for example, those in the organisation Potential and the group of entrepreneurs on the right bank of the Dnepr. However, the interests of various societal groups are generally hardly represented at the political level.

Zaporizhzhya society is fragmented and everybody keeps information for himself. This fragmentation inhibits information flows and hampers an open debate about necessary changes. This contributes to an ossification of social and economic structures. Fragmentation inhibits horizontal co-operation that may enable innovation processes to develop. Lack of transparency and open discussion makes collective learning, essential in socio-economic progress, very difficult.

Given the weakness of the state and civil society, an integrational vacuum at all levels developed in Zaporizhzhya after the disintegration of the party-state that kept society and economy together. This was the case in Tsarist times when society was atomised in a similar way.

A factor of Zaporizhzhya society is its typical class structure. In Zaporizhzhya one can find a large, amorphous and little-educated working class. This makes Zaporizhzhya a proletarian town where political power is exercised in a way that is more crude than in most other Ukrainian towns. A middle class hardly exists in Zaporizhzhya and the tiny cultural intelligentsia functions in limbo, largely cut off from economic and political life. The traditional attitude of the intelligentsia is to stay away from power.

Behavioural routines of the ruling elite

Behavioural routines of the present ruling elite of Zaporizhzhya are formed in communist times and not much affected by foreign influences. Erosion of communist ideology and ossification of social and political structures over the past decades has developed an elite that is not interested anymore in the development of society and economy. The aim is to control society and economy to its own benefit. Power is a major aim in itself as with it material wealth can be accumulated. Power is the key to all other attributes that are important in society (see Appendix 1).

In former times, the public interest was of overriding importance, at least in official ideology; nowadays, the public interest does not play any role. Political and public life seem to have become privatised. 'Jungle individualism' has replaced collectivism as an ideology. This means that the political and economic elite in Zaporizhzhya acts as a predatory class.

The ruling elite of Zaporizhzhya may have travelled abroad, but usually only knows the surface of developed market economies. Moreover, it is very difficult to learn in Zaporizhzhya about developments outside the Community of Independent States.[7] This limited knowledge of the outside

Box 3.1 Newsmedia: no crisis in Zaporizhzhya

When reading Zaporizhzhya newspapers, one does not have the impression that people are hungry, that half of the population is unemployed, that society at large is in disarray and the economy is in free fall. Nobody knows from the newspapers that cultural life has collapsed, that pensioners live in deep poverty and that houses are decaying. You are panicking about the situation? Journalists are not. They are interviewing the director of Zaporozhstal and they are convinced that everything is in harmony. In general, life became better and merrier. Everything is OK. The truth is never written down, although it once was. During 1991 - 1992, a flood of information flooded out to the local population, by local newspapers. Even in 1993 one wrote critically about the situation in health care and education. Since then, when reading articles about schools and hospitals, about problems of disabled and unemployed and about the survival strategies of the population, one would grind one's teeth.

Among the local newspapers, at the level of chief editors and permanent staff, a tacit agreement now exists not to write against each other and not to quarrel. Almost no one subscribes to newspapers, out of the conviction that tomorrow there may be no money for bread. Therefore newspapers are distributed on the streets, mostly by the unemployed and pensioners. Those who buy newspapers instead of bread, expect with fervour something interesting. If one takes into account that books are hardly sold anymore, that libraries are rare and one has to reach them by expensive public transport and that Moscow's television programmes are selectively broadcasted and shown at unconvenient hours, then newspapers become almost the only rescue from the daily information vacuum.

The press is half dead. Renumeration for journalists is miserable. And, honestly speaking, one can not give much for the style of most journalists. Even if one journalist has an inspiring piece, the pen of the chief editor will take the best sections immediately away.

The offical radio stations virtually disappeared for most inhabitants of Zaporizhzhya with the appearance of private channels like 'Nostalgia', 'Radio Saga' or 'Big Bow', the latter one the most popular among the Zaporizhzhia radio stations. These commercial stations succeeded in attracting the largest share of audience but do not inform them. The stations feature informal and relaxed intercourse with listeners, live-broadcasted, popular music but no serious news.

The former popularity of foreign radio stations, like Deutsche Welle, BBC and the Voice of America, declined when it became allowed to listen to them. In times of Glasnost, local politics, seen by the local population as a bone in the throat, was not interesting - people were tired with it, and preoccupied with feeding their children and surviving up to the next salary payment.

On the commercial TV channels, like Hortitsa and Aleks, TV5 one can hear about the bitter truth of daily life in Zaporizhzhya. Although one can quickly forget it when looking at American thrillers at the same channels.

All in all, people in Zaporizhzhya have access to eight channels, but far from everyone has the opportunity to see all programmes, due, above all, to bad antennes and television sets. People do not have money for better equipment. Most inhabitants, living in poverty, do not even have the money to repair a defect television set, let alone buy a new one. If the TV still works, in many cases one has to be satisfied with the reception of the offical stations and Hortitsa.

The personal freedom of reporters and editors of the official station Zaporizhzhya depend on the local political power and the non-payment of salary over months. Personnel of commercial stations have more freedom, but they are restrained by lack of experience.

The Kyiv stations UT and UT-2 do not give any information about Zaporizhzhya. They broadcast in Ukrainian, mostly on a very low level.

Then there is the channel KVN. During last years its level declined continuously. This channel has some satirical programmes, but it is difficult to laugh with a empty stomach especially if the political direction in its satire dissappeared. Glasnost has ended in the capital and was not able to unfold in the province.

world, including the experiences of other post-socialist countries, lead to many naive assumptions about the combination of elements of centrally planned and market economy. The ruling elite does not know anything about the functioning of the regional economy and the causes of the present crisis. The redistributive syndrome (see Chapter 2) that they help to preserve contributes to a downward economic mechanism that erodes the power base of the ruling elite. It seems that the ruling elite of Zaporizhzhya rules in ignorance and splendid isolation.

One of the major legacies of communism is the sphere of secrecy around those who govern. Even the most elementary information has not been made public. The bulletin of the Zaporizhzhya Statistical Office is considered as classified material. No statistical booklet about Zaporizhzhya is publicly available.[8] Related to this secrecy, the unwillingness to give information and the intolerance towards independent analyses, is the fact that over the last ten years only one analysis of the regional economy and society of Zaporizhzhya has been published.[9] Information is considered as power and not something to give freely away. This attitude contributes to the phenomenon that Zaporizhzhya society is a myriad of small groups, families and clans that hardly communicate with each other. Related to this is the absence of public debate. Moreover, a widespread distrust exists that considerably enhances transaction costs within the economy.

Apparently, within the ruling elite the adage still exists that who is not with them, is against them. The rulers are mostly not conscious of this specific way of ruling that is handed over from one generation to another in 'silent' ways.[10] This traditional way of ruling seems incompatible with modern ways of governing state and economy.

A suffocating bureaucracy

The bureaucracy of both the municipality and province function in the tradition of Russian and Soviet bureaucracy, characterised by utterly unfriendly behaviour towards clients and the obstacles they create for economic development. According to interviewees, in Zaporizhzhya these characteristics seem to be even more pronounced compared to most other Ukrainian towns.

The bureaucracy exhibits a control mania but is at the same time not much concerned about the outcome of bureaucratic action. A lot of energy is spent, on all levels, at defending bureaucratic competencies as well as by senior bureaucrats in delineating their domains with respect to that of others.

There hardly seems to be any delegation of competencies. It seems that the bureaucracy sees itself as a goal in itself. A corollary is a very low degree of competence, for example, this kind of bureaucracy has great difficulties in taking decisions. If decisions are taken, they are taken on a high level and often informally. There is a low public service ethos, that is, there is little concern for the public interest in preference to private and sectoral interests and a feeling of public accountability is absent. There is no regard for the law. Another characteristic of Zaporizhzhya bureaucracy is the lack of information flowing amongst the various bureaucratic departments. Bureaucratic structures are very hierarchical where top-down information flows are predominating.

The state bureaucracy constitutes a cornerstone in the power structure of Zaporizhzhya. Here, private interests of bureaucrats and their control mania paralyses the whole functioning of society and economy. Nobody can circumvent the bureaucracy and good relationships with bureaucrats, including bribes, is a *sine qua non* for success in public life.[11]

The middle, non-competent layers of the bureaucracy constitute an especially formidable obstacle for a reform of any kind. However, a modern economy needs a facilitative and a symbiotic bureaucracy rather than a parasitic bureaucracy.

A new element has been introduced in the relationship between bureaucracy and population. As the financial crisis of local authorities deepened, the municipality tried to charge as much as possible to the general population. To begin with, the larger portion of real costs for consumed energy, housing services and public transport were charged to the population. On the other hand, new taxes were imposed. As most people cannot afford to pay more for public services and houses, they simply stopped paying rents and payments for several services. As only a small part of planned income is realised, public authorities react by raising prices and rents even more. Therefore, people get more indebted. This process results in a gradual sharpening of the relationship between local bureaucracy and population as the local bureaucracy increasingly is faced with payments arrears. They may, for example, cut the warm water supply or sell the houses of people that do not pay their rent.

Conclusion

The Byzantine way in which political power functions in Zaporizhzhya furthers incompetence rather than competence. Politicians usually do not have any idea about the causes of the present crisis and the way to solve it. The attitude of the leadership of large state enterprises and town and provincial administration is to wait and see. The ruling elite acts like a predatory class that is not at all interested in social and economic development. Parliamentary democracy is mainly a facade for the continuation of authoritarian rule; it is a reminder, in many respects, of tsarist times.

Societal interests are hardly represented at the political level. There seems to be a big divide between the ruling elite and the impoverished and desperate masses of the population.

Notes

1. Nomenklature is the name for the communist caste that ruled the Soviet Union. Influential posts could only be granted if the candidate was admitted to the Nomenklature ranks.
2. In 1990 14,400 persons were working in the state administration (municipalities and province), while in 1996 it were 27,000 (Zaporizke 1997b).
3. The socio-economic system of Tsarist Russia can not be labelled as feudal. Feudalism in its institutional meaning is only applicable to Western Europe. In a broader sense it involves a structure of personal dependence, rights over property corresponding to such dependence, and a fragmentation of political authority.
4. This assessment is based primarily on interviews with persons that are knowledgeable about the behaviour of these new groupings.
5. Dornberg, p. 96, 98.
6. Fifty per cent has been a critical threshold if less than half the population voted, new elections had to be organised.
7. Foreign newspapers and periodicals, other than Russian ones, are not available in Zaporizhzhya, neither in the shops nor in the libraries. Ukrainian newspapers, that are generally of very low quality, hardly report about developments outside the former Soviet Union. It is practically impossible for an inhabitant of Zaporizhzhya to become acquainted with major works of sociology or economy, if not translated in Russian or Ukrainian. Book shops have a very poor assortment of literature. Under Gorbachev's rule it had been no problem to buy foreign newspapers in Zaporizhzhya.
8. In communist times there was more openness. Then sometimes statistical books about Zaporizhzhya region have been published.
9. That is Semonov, Spencer Pierce.
10. This can be considered as 'tacit knowledge'.
11. According to the periodial *Ekonomika Ukraina*, the average senior official in Ukraine earns 60 per cent of his income by bribes.

4 The Ukrainisation of Zaporizhzhya

The Russification of Zaporizhzhya

Traditionally, Zaporizhzhya belonged to the Ukrainian lands. However, the language of the ruling elite has for ages been Russian, as these lands were part of the Russian empire. Most town dwellers were Russian speaking. School education in towns has mostly been in Russian, which has always been the gateway to world culture.

During the nineteenth century, nationalism developed among the Ukrainian intelligentsia that comprised a tiny part of the urban population, mainly in the western part of Ukraine. However, they were deeply rooted in Russian culture and the greater part of them did not opt for an independent Ukraine. The Ukrainian nobility believed they had more in common with other nobles than with their fellow countrymen.

During the 1920s and 1930s, the use of Ukrainian culture and language expanded, as the policy of the Communist Party at that time was to stimulate national cultures and languages. In the countryside of Zaporizhzhya most schools used and are still using Ukrainian as the teaching language. However, especially after World War II, a russification campaign gained force, related to the incorporation of some western Ukrainian provinces into the Soviet Union.

The industrialisation drive that had begun under Stalin has meant for Ukraine that the industrial centre of gravity shifted to the South East of Ukraine. Mainly Russian speakers moved to the rapidly developing towns of the South-east, among them Zaporizhzhya. As a result the proportion of Russians in Ukraine increased from 7 per cent to about 22 per cent between 1926 and 1989. In the South-east this shift was much more pronounced.

Ukrainian nationalism has its strongest roots in Western Ukraine, especially those provinces that had been part of the Austrian empire (Western Galicia, Bukovina and Transcarpathia). Under German occupation, Ukrainian nationalism gained force and allied itself partially with the German occupiers. Until 1952 a Ukrainian guerrilla resistance was active in Western Ukraine.

The Communist Party has always been keen to oppress nationalist groupings and tendencies in Ukraine, given the strategic significance of Ukraine. Under the rule of Brezhnev, coming from Ukraine himself, numerous Ukrainian nationalist dissidents were persecuted. In Zaporizhzhya, during the 1970s lecturers in Ukrainian and Ukrainian history were dismissed due to nationalist tendencies. During the 1980s, Ukrainian nationalists gathered around the nationalist Ruch party, with strong roots in the West Ukrainian intelligentsia.

Sometimes the party leadership was inclined to give in to demands of Ukrainians. For example, in the early 1970s Ukrainian intellectuals, also from Zaporizhzhya, asked the Ministry of Culture in Kyiv to build a monument for the memory of Zaporizhzhya Sitch. Money was already collected and preparations for the building had begun. Then, in 1971, Shelest was removed as party leader of Ukraine and the whole project was blocked. The whole idea was associated with Ukrainian nationalism as, traditionally, they saw in Zaporizhzhya Sitch the roots of the Ukrainian nation.

According to the census of 1989, 32 per cent of the population of Zaporizhzhya province are Russians. However, many Ukrainians speak Russian as their first language. In Eastern Ukraine as a whole, Ukrainian-speaking Ukrainians only accounted for 44 per cent of the population.[1] Most individuals in Zaporizhzhya province have multiple ethnic identifications. According to the 1989 census, 10 per cent of all marriages in Zaporizhzhya province are mixed marriages, 42 per cent all Ukrainian and about 40 per cent Russian[2]. The overwhelming majority of people in the town of Zaporizhzhya speak Russian while in the countryside most people speak Ukrainian.

The Ukrainisation of Zaporizhzhya

Independence came in 1991 more or less as a gift. It came about primarily because the ruling elites in the Soviet republics thought their interests would be better protected in the case of dissolution of the Soviet Union.

A handful of Soviet republics had already declared independence in 1990. On 16 July 1990 a declaration of economic and political sovereignty of Ukraine had been accepted by the Ukrainian parliament. In the March

1991 referendum 80 per cent of the Ukrainian population voted to stay within a new Soviet Union of sovereign states on the basis of the 1990 sovereignty declaration.[3] After the aborted putsch in Moscow of August 1991 the Ukrainian parliament declared Ukraine's total independence. This was approved by the population in a referendum that took place on 1 December 1991 - 91 per cent of the population voted for total independence.[4]

In the period just before independence radical nationalists in Zaporizhzhya issued leaflets stating that the key to prosperity of the Ukrainian nation would be independence. They wrote about large transfers from Ukraine to the centre. Their judgements did not take into account the disruptive effects of the disintegration of the highly integrated Soviet economy. Most of the Russian-speaking intelligentsia in Zaporizhzhya tended to believe the naive assumptions of the nationalists.

It is from this perspective that the support for independence during the 1991 referendum in Zaporizhzhya can be explained, as well as the fact that just after the aborted coup attempt in Moscow, trust in the political process at the national level was very low. Nevertheless, support for independence was unstable and unreliable.

The re-orientation from Moscow to Kyiv

After independence, the fact that a new state has been created set in motion a dynamic that had several disruptive effects. The new government and state bureaucracy did not have any experience in governing a country and the needed institutions were not in place. Also, the new state needed a justification, a *raison d'etre*. This was a problem given the fact that there was hardly a historical precedent for a Ukrainian state. Moreover, the older generation of nationalists, who had played an important role in the formation of the Ukrainian nation, had a pre-industrial view of what constitutes a nation and were primarily interested in the symbols of the new state, like the national anthem.

In the first phase of independence, the Ukrainian government actively supported the disruption of economic links with Russia. For example, Ukraine began to levy value-added tax on imports and exports, including those from and to Russia. In 1991 Ukraine's inter-republican trade amounted to 60 per cent of its total output.[5] The disruption of economic links with the other republics of the former Soviet Union in 1992 has been considered the single biggest cause of Ukraine's 20 per cent production decline in that year. During the first years of independence it was mainly the import of Russian oil and gas and the export of Ukrainian sugar that was affected by the dissolution of the Soviet Union.[6]

Nevertheless, in the first phase of independence, in many respects, relations between Ukraine and Russia went on as usual, despite government policies. However, after some years it appeared that traditional markets in Russia were lost. For example, it became very difficult for Avtozaz to sell their bad-quality cars to Russia. In Soviet times, most of its production went to Russia. Also, the price of imported Russian oil and gas increased enormously. In the first phase of independence it was often difficult to find alternatives for the supplies from Russia that were not available any more due to shortages. Later, from 1994-1995 onwards, the bad debt problem appeared, involving a chain of debts among enterprises. Russian enterprises were often no longer willing to deliver to non-paying clients in Ukraine and vice versa. This meant that trade between Zaporizhzhya province and the other republics of the former Soviet Union was decimated. By 1996 exports to Russia as a percentage of total exports of Zaporizhzhya has declined to 28 per cent.

The Ukrainisation of Zaporizhzhya meant in the first instance a rupture of relations with Moscow, the centre of the Russian and Soviet empire and a re-orientation of relations towards Kyiv, the capital of the new state. Also, gradually, relations between inhabitants of Zaporizhzhya and their friends and family in Russia became more difficult. In the first years of independence this had not been felt immediately but gradually more barriers against the free movement of goods and citizens were established. This caused a major rupture in the history of Zaporizhzhya province.

How the Ukrainisation campaign was implemented

The Ukrainisation of Zaporizhzhya also implied the imposition of a new nationalist ideology.

Immediately after independence new history books were introduced in the schools. In 1992, children in secondary schools in Zaporizhzhya learned from history books published in the German-occupied Western Ukraine in the early 1940s. In these text books Ukrainians who had killed a lot of Russians were glorified. No one protested that all schools in Zaporizhzhya were taught from these books even though they have been in the meantime replaced by other history books, though they are not much better. Nowadays, schoolchildren in Zaporizhzhya learn that the Ukrainian nation is the root of all other Slavic nations and that the Russian language developed from the Ukrainian language. They also learn that the Ukrainian nation developed out of the ancient Greek nation.

The Ukrainisation of Zaporizhzhya province also meant an imposed use of Ukrainian as an official language and the concomitant efforts to marginalise Russian in official and everyday life although Russian is spoken by most citizens of Zaporizhzhya town. Officials from state institutions, are obliged to answer the telephone in Ukrainian. Official documents are in Ukrainian even though it costs a lot of money to translate documents from Russian into Ukrainian.

Paradoxically, the shift towards the Ukrainian language especially posed problems for the Russian speaking Ukrainians many of whom had dropped the study of Ukrainian when the discipline became facultative at school in the late 1970s. Although they often had the ability to read Ukrainian, they did not have the ability to write Ukrainian. Suddenly they, and others who did not master Ukrainian, found themselves in a difficult position when applying for jobs in the state sector where knowledge of Ukrainian was required. Suddenly, in 1991, Ukrainian became obligatory again in Russian schools and those who had dropped Ukrainian at an earlier stage, came in for great difficulties when faced with an examination in Ukrainian when leaving school.

In schools Russian suddenly has become for Russian-speaking school children a foreign language. Ukrainian schools have spread and by early 1997 constituted about half of all secondary schools in Zaporizhzhya town. Elite schools are still Russian but the Ministry of Education has offered salary increases for those elite schools that will turn into Ukrainian schools.

The teaching of Russian literature has also been marginalised and very little time is now spent on Russian classical writers like Tolstoy, Dostoyevski and Lermontov. Teachers of Russian literature became teachers of foreign literature. Only a few elite schools have the right to put Russian on the curriculum.

By early 1997, at the local state university it had been decided that the faculty of Russian language and literature would be abolished and lecturers in this speciality transferred to the department of Roman and German languages. During the early 1990s there were annually approximately about 75 students that chose Russian language and literature. Nowadays this number has fallen to approximately 15 to 25 students. Teachers of Russian language and literature face unemployment.

The process of Ukrainisation described above means more or less a break with the main access to world culture in general. The Ukrainian intelligentsia used to express itself in Russian and major literary figures from Ukraine, such as Bulgakov and Gogol, wrote in Russian. Moreover, as the Ukrainian language had been oppressed for such a long time, it had not developed into a sophisticated instrument of communication in science and culture. Therefore, the Ukrainian language lacks the richness that makes Russian a world language. The marginalisation of Russian language and culture therefore means a marginalisation of culture in general.

Why do school directors execute the most absurd orders from above? Because they are afraid not to do so. School directors can be dismissed whenever the municipal authorities want. So, they are eager to execute any order from above. The directors do not heed protests against Ukrainisation. Then the question is to explain the docile mentality of public authorities in Zaporizhzhya that implement all measures coming from Kyiv. This seems to run counter to the interests of the Russian-speaking ruling elite in Zaporizhzhya who are sending their children to the Russian speaking elite schools. However, those who act as dictators in their own domain, act as slaves with regard to authorities in Kyiv, even more so compared to other towns in Eastern Ukraine

Most inhabitants of Zaporizhzhya are informed about world events, and events in their own country, by the Russian mass media, especially television. This is not only because the majority of inhabitants of Zaporizhzhya are Russian speaking, but also because they consider the Russian media to be of better quality. One of the steps in the Ukrainisation campaign was to make Russian newspapers and books more expensive. Another step, in October 1996, was to reduce the broadcasting of ORT, the Russian TV channel for the whole of the former Soviet Union. The authorities continued to allow the broadcasting of the least interesting programmes. This was an order from Kyiv, immediately followed up by the Zaporizhzhya administration, even though it was not carried out in Kharkiv. Also, the Zaporizhzhya provincial administration decided to introduce Ukrainian as the only official language, while the municipality in Kharkiv decided that both Russian and Ukrainian were official languages.[7] It points to the docile mentality of Zaporizhzhya political leaders.[8]

Russians are increasingly denied basic rights. Ukraine is herewith violating documents it has signed in the past, including documents signed when becoming a member of the Council of Europe. Relations between the language groups are regulated by the Law on Languages which gives persons belonging to an ethnic minority the right to study and receive information in his/her language.[9]

It is strange that this Ukrainisation campaign is implemented despite the fact that the majority of Ukraine is Russian speaking and that the leading stratum in Kyiv is mainly from Eastern Ukraine and Russian speaking (the Dnipropetrovsk clan), and notwithstanding the fact that the ruling elite of Zaporizhzhya is Russian speaking. It is partly a reflection of weak counter forces in Zaporizhzhya society and partly a reflection of the fragility of the new Ukrainian state and nation. Ukraine never has existed as an independent nation. The very existence of Ukraine has very weak foundations: it is not well inserted in the European security system, it is economically very weak, it has no natural borders and a larger part of the population is attracted to neighbouring nations.

Conclusion

Since the independence of Ukraine was declared in December 1991, Zaporizhzhya suddenly re-oriented all relations to Kyiv, the new capital. This meant a major turning-point in the history of Zaporizhzhya and disrupted many economic links, family ties and cultural relations.

The Ukrainisation campaign in Zaporizhzhya that started in 1991 has assumed dramatic proportions in this predominantly Russian speaking town. The Russian speaking majority has become a discriminated 'minority'. The campaign has contributed to a marginalisation of culture and an alienation of the majority of the population with respect to their government. The Ukrainisation campaign has been implemented without any protests from the part of the population. However, it contains the seeds for future conflict.

Notes

1. Kuzio, Wilson, p. 33 During the nineteenth century in South-eastern Ukraine only 2.7 per cent of all marriages were mixed marriages.
2. Pirie, p. 1086.
3. In Ukraine 74 per cent of the population voted yes when asked March 1991 'Do you consider it necessary to preserve the Union of Soviet Socialist Republics as a

renewed federation of equal sovereign republics in which human rights and the freedom of all nationalities will be fully guaranteed?' (*Economist*, 23 March 1991).

4. On 9 December 1991 Ukraine, Russia and Belarus formed the Community of Independent States. In the same month all other former Union republics, except the Baltic states, joined.
5. *Economist*, 1 February 1992.
6. In 1992 Russian oil exports to Ukraine went down by 25 per cent compared to 1991, whereas Ukrainian sugar exports to Russia declined by 60 per cent (*Economist,* 13 February 1993).
7. 10 January 1997, ITAR-TASS press agency. BBC world broadcasting service. Also Donetsk, with almost 80 per cent Russian speakers, decided to use only Ukrainian in office work.
8. Western institutions also often help in this Ukrainisation campaign. When the German Friedrich Ebert Foundation organised in March 1997 in Zaporizhzhya a seminar about leadership in politics for political parties, the invitation was issued in Russian. But the whole seminar was in Ukrainian, so excluding a lot of Russian-speaking politicians.
9. Article 10 of Section 1 of the Constitution of Ukraine proclaims 'the state (official) language of Ukraine is Ukrainian. In the areas of dense concentration of citizens, who are part of one or several national minorities, the language acceptable for the majority of residents of that specific populated region may be used in addition to the state language in the activity of bodies of state power and of state organisations.' According to the Human Development Report of the United Nations Office in Ukraine, almost 17 million people, or every third Ukrainian citizen, has Russian as its first language, including 11.4 million Russians.

5 The De-industrialisation of Zaporizhzhya

This chapter is about change in industrial Zaporizhzhya, especially since independence of Ukraine. First, the eight largest enterprises, that form the economic base of Zaporizhzhya, will be described separately. Subsequently, the most important industrial sectors will be discussed.

The character of industrial enterprises in Zaporizhzhya

Big enterprises in Zaporizhzhya are characterised by a high degree of self-support and by a wide range of activities and services for employees. Because in the centrally planned economy nearly everything was in shortage, enterprises tried to produce as many things as possible themselves and had large reserves of inputs. In Zaporizhzhya a high share of enterprises functioned under the responsibility of all-Union ministries. It was only in 1991 that directors took over control from the branch ministries in Moscow. The result was relatively few links amongst the enterprises of Zaporizhzhya.

In contradistinction with most big enterprises in the developed market economies (Japan is a case apart), here enterprises often run (part of) a town. It means that they take care of the whole infrastructure of the part of town they own. For example, Zaporozhstal, the main steel producer, has a network of health care facilities, educational establishments, guest houses, kindergartens, apartments, cultural facilities, sport clubs and holiday centres. Zaporozhstal also has two kolkhozes, mainly, but not only, producing for its employees. It even has a meat factory within the steel factory. Often, these secondary services are more important for the employees than the salary.

Usually, the factory could mediate in the provision of scarce goods. The factory also has shops that are open to the larger public. For example, Zaporozhstal provides about 5 per cent of all goods traded in retail trade in Zaporizhzhya.[1] Moreover there are sideline products, that often have nothing to do with the main product and that are sold to the wider public. Under Gorbachev, the production of sideline consumer goods was stimulated, as these goods were scarce. For many enterprises, this sideline production has become more important as the demand for mainline products declined sharply.

This means that the large enterprises in Zaporizhzhya have many more employees than a comparable enterprise in the West that produces the same amount of mainline products. The lower labour productivity of the Zaporizhzhya workers should also be taken into account when explaining the high level of employment.

Of course, in the new conditions of the market economy, this organisational structure of big enterprises is an obstacle to privatisation and restructuring, although there is a trend of economising on the social activities. However, there is no organisational restructuring of the sideline activities. Though, sometimes they are made independent.

The Ukrainian government has made a decision to transfer the social sphere of enterprises to the local administration. However, no legal base for such a transfer has yet been created and in the current privatisation process, usually big enterprises include their social infrastructure when being privatised.

The social sphere has become an increasing burden. Also, a greater number of non-employees have made greater use of these services, often without payment.[2]

Hindrances to restructuring also have deeper, socio-political roots. The enterprise's organisation is along hierarchical lines, with the enterprise director acting like a patriarch (the 'red director'). Semi-feudal relations can be found that recall pre-Revolutionary Russia and Ukraine.[3] For example, the workers' collective of Avtozaz had an agreement with the board of directors that no strikes will be organised.[4] It is also in this context that dismissal of personnel is quite difficult for a lot of enterprises.

The picture sketched above of a typical Zaporizhzhya big enterprise shows the deficiencies of a typical mainstream economic analysis and the need for a comprehensive socio-economic approach to the restructuring of big enterprises.

In this chapter the eight largest enterprises, that have, officially, 94,000 employees altogether, will be analysed.

Heavy metallurgy

Heavy metallurgy constitutes the base of the industrial complex of Zaporizhzhya. In many ways the government supported this branch, especially under President Kravchuk.[5] Due to lack of monetary transparency it is difficult to assess profitability and prospects of these enterprises. Generally, in Ukraine the capacities of the steel plants are far too large for domestic needs. The Soviet economy used to be very energy- and material-intensive. Thus, even when former income levels are attained again, need for steel will be less. Especially during transition domestic consumption of steel dropped, more than the average decline of demand. Therefore, reliance upon exports has become very great.

Table 5.1 Production and exports of iron and steel, Zaporizhzhya province, 1990 - 1997

	1990	1991	1992	1994	1995	1996	1997*
production of iron (1000 tonnes)	3973	3092	3006	2028	1734	2110	1166
production of steel (1000 tonnes)	5253	4597	4163	2764	2536	2819	1696
rolled iron (1000 tonnes)	3448	3134	2962	2216	1953	2299	1358
export of iron (1000 tonnes)		98	194	76	1201		
exports of iron alloys (1000 tonnes)		27	69	239	233		
exports of steel (1000 tonnes)		234	193	484	701		
export of heavy metals (1000 $)				315,469	413,230	531,339	340,407

* first half year

Source: Zaporizhzhya Statistical Office

The table shows how much the steel industry, especially iron production (Zaporozhstal), has become dependent on exports. It is due to these exports that the relative weight of ferrous metallurgy in Ukrainian economy has increased. In early 1995, the share of heavy industry, including basic chemicals and energy sector, attained 59 per cent of industrial production from less than 30 per cent at the end of the 1980s.[6]

Generally, production outlays have become outdated, while investments are at a very low level, which makes prospects for profitability of exports quite gloomy.[7] However, these prospects differ greatly among the three major steel plants.

Zaporozhstal and Dneprospetsstal

Zaporozhstal and Dneprospetsstal are the two leading steel enterprises in Zaporizhzhya.

Zaporozhstal is the flagship of heavy metallurgy in South-eastern Ukraine and the fourth largest metallurgical enterprise in Ukraine. Zaporozhstal has an ageing management that has done little to modernise the plant but gained a lot by exporting. By mid-1996 only 15-20 per cent of production was for the domestic market. Zaporozhstal sells a lot in barter deals for which it receives coal and electric energy in return.[8] In 1995, exports were mainly to China (35 per cent), Russia (13 per cent), other parts of the former Soviet Union (14 per cent) and Turkey (9 per cent). However, foreign markets are unstable. For example, whereas in 1995 44 per cent of exports went to China, in 1994 the percentage was 7 per cent and in 1993 23.5 per cent.[9] Since 1996, when Russia began to tax imports from Ukraine by 20 per cent, exports to Russia have declined and have become less profitable.

Iron is produced in open-hearth furnaces (Martin ovens), constructed in the 1930s and which are very energy-intensive. These plants use per unit of iron twice as much energy as modern steel mills. Therefore, these open-hearth furnaces can not compete on the world market if real costs were reflected in prices. Due to rising energy prices, prices of Zaparozhstal are already close to the world market level. The quality of steel from Zaporozhstal is very low. According to reports on the steel industry in Central Europe, it is the production of low-quality steels that is the least profitable.[10] Given the above mentioned circumstantial evidence, it seems unlikely that Zaporozhstal will survive without government support.

Dneprospetsstal is an electrometallurgical enterprise, profiting from the neighbouring Zaporizhzhya hydroelectric power plant. It is producing high-quality steels and in co-operation with Western firms, certification has been introduced. However, clients in the West considered it not to be high quality due to too low a purity. This low purity is caused by the non-mechanical mixing of inputs. This factory needs to be modernised although equipment is less outdated than that of Zaporozhstal. Diversification of products is extremely important for the firm. Although having better prospects than Zaporozhstal, the problem of survival has been posed in the press. The share of exports in total production was only 10 per cent of total production in 1994, in 1995 this percentage became 50 per cent. In the first nine months of

1995, exports were mainly to Belgium (43 per cent), Slovakia (16 per cent), Romania (12.5 per cent) and Russia (10 per cent).[11]

Low share of domestic demand is also related to unwillingness to deliver to domestic clients. A local private entrepreneur wanted to buy a large amount of steel from Dneprospetsstal. However, Dneprospetsstal was not willing to supply and could not fix a price. The entrepreneur assumed that this was related to the fact that the cost price of steel is not known to the enterprise and that domestic delivery entails more financial risks than supplies abroad.

Light metallurgy

Major enterprises within light metallurgy are Ferrosplavzavod, Magnesium and Titanium Enterprise and Aluminium Enterprise.

Ferrosplavzavod

This factory is, together with a factory in Nikopol, in Zaporizhzhya province, a monopolist in the field of manganese alloys, without which it is impossible to produce high-quality steels. All the important raw materials are found in the region: quartz, manganese, cokes. For this factory, co-operation with Russia is essential. Metals are made with help of electrothermical processes. The factory was built in 1953 and since then has been modernised several times. This factory has a relatively young management. According to Coopers and Lybrand 1993, this factory is one of the few that may be profitable in the current critical circumstances. However, all the factors that contributed to a low cost price in 1993 (low price of electrical energy, low labour costs, low price of raw materials and good exchange rate) had disappeared by 1997. Moreover, during the last few years the factory has been faced, like all others, with cuts in the delivery of electric energy.

Forty-eight per cent of exports were to Russia, 16 per cent to Switzerland, 9 per cent to Ireland, 8 per cent to Germany and 7 per cent to England in the first nine months of 1995.[12]

Magnesium and Titanium Enterprise[13]

This enterprise was founded in 1956. Titanium, magnesium, germanium and silicon are produced here. In the former Soviet Union, there were two other, similar factories, in the Ural and Kazakhstan. The enterprise mainly produced for the military industrial complex. In 1992, 5 per cent of the world production of titanium and magnesium was produced in this enterprise.[14] Silicon is used for aircraft, airspace, medical equipment, computers and microelectronics. There is a high demand on the world market for the products produced by the enterprise. However, the enterprise came into great difficulties after the disintegration of the former Soviet Union and the economic crisis in Ukraine. An additional problem was that prices for silicon declined sharply on the world market in the 1990 - 1993 period. In 1996, the production of silicon has dropped to 20 per cent of the factory's capacity and that of germanium to 30 per cent of the factory's capacity.

Seventy per cent of titanium was used by the Soviet military industrial complex; the collapse of this complex contributed to the problems of the enterprise.[15] Export of titanium declined from 2105 kg in 1994, to 850 kg in 1995 to 27 kg during the first half of 1996.[16]

The purity of products is not high enough, prices are too high to compete and production technology is completely outdated. In addition, the 'strategic nature' of the enterprise prevented foreign direct investment in the first phase of transition.

In Ukraine this enterprise is a monopoly. Magnesium ore is found in Zaporizhzhya province and titanium in the neighbouring province of Dnipropretovsk and in Lviv. Despite a special 'titanium - programme' of the government, the personnel of the enterprise declined from 7500 persons in 1991 to 2000 in early 1996. The laboratory, where 190 scientists used to work, has been closed. The production of titanium has been stopped.

However, a titanium institute, independent from the enterprise, is still functioning.[17]

In order to produce on world market level, investments are needed. If there are no foreign investments, the whole enterprise will be closed.

Aluminium Enterprise

The Aluminium Enterprise is the main aluminium factory in Ukraine. It used to produce mainly for the aviation industry, which is now in crisis. Ukraine had to import three-quarters of all the aluminium it needed.[18] Nevertheless, the Aluminium Enterprise exported a large percentage of its production due to the fact that a lot of domestic clients could not pay and that the factory needed hard currency to modernise. Modernisation is urgently needed as production outlays, based on the Soderberg method, are completely outdated.

Moreover, equipment is very dangerous for the workers and production methods are very polluting. Due to high pollution levels, Aluminium Enterprise could not get a trading license for the London Stock Exchange.[19]

In 1995 the Aluminium Enterprise accounted for 15.4 per cent of all exports of Zaporizhzhya province. Exports are mainly to the USA (76 per cent), and Russia (16 per cent).[20] Exports went up from 56.8 million dollars in 1994 to 117.6 million dollars in 1996 to 60.8 million dollars in the first half of 1997.

Whereas formerly bauxite came from the former Soviet Union, nowadays this raw material is imported from Africa and Latin America. In 1992, bauxite has been delivered for an average price of 46-52 dollars per tonne, whereas competitors in Western Europe had bauxite for 25-35 dollars per tonne.[21] All other raw materials come from Ukraine, except electrodes and nickel.

Forty per cent of production costs consist of electrical energy. Per tonne of aluminium, Aluminium Enterprise uses 21.5 per cent more energy than its Western competitors.[22] Aluminium is of low quality with a high iron content. For that reason lower prices must be accepted. Nowadays, modernisation of the firm is effectuated with the assistance of an American firm, Ford Daniel.

In recent years the competitiveness of this enterprise declined drastically with rising energy prices (increase by a factor of 10 in dollar terms in the period March 1993 - March 1996) and rising labour costs (increase by a factor of 13 in dollar terms in the period March 1993 - December 1995).[23] In 1993, wages accounted for 8.3 dollars per tonne of produced aluminium, while the corresponding figure for the average Western aluminium producer has been 135 dollars. By the end of 1995, in Zaporizhzhya wages accounted for about 108 dollars per tonne of produced aluminium.

Sideline production, such as venetian blinds and building materials, has been developed, mainly based on aluminium.

Transformerzavod

This factory produced, in Soviet times, high-power transformers for the whole of the former Soviet Union and was the only producer of these big transformers. It used to be the largest producer of transformers in the world, but much of the equipment is outdated. There is a high level of vertical integration - most of the inputs the factory needs are produced within the factory. Inputs mainly consist of raw materials. Since the collapse of the

Soviet Union production has declined steeply. By mid-1997, the factory was working at about 30 per cent of its capacity. However, no personnel has been fired.

Transformerzavod had a big research institute that employed 1800 engineers. By the mid-1990s, this institute had become independent and most of its personnel had been fired.

In 1991 about 10 per cent of production was for export, while in 1996 - 1997 it was between 50 and 60 per cent, of which 40 per cent for exports to the 'far abroad', mainly to China, Argentine, Morocco, Egypt and Greece.

Since the collapse of the Soviet Union product differentiation has started and the factory now also produces small transformers as well as generators. The factory has representations in various countries. Through all these channels they try to react on tenders.

There are liquidity problems and clients are usually asked to pay 20 per cent in advance. Clients in Ukraine are required to pay the entire fee in advance. In the first years after independence there were problems with clients in the former Soviet Union who were not credit-worthy. Trade with Russia is usually in roubles or in barter deals.

Avtozaz

Avtozaz was founded in 1961 in order to produce cheap cars for the whole of the Soviet Union and was in this category a monopoly. Other car factories, like the Lada factory in Togliatti, got a priority treatment. With the independence of Ukraine, Avtozaz became in 1991 the only manufacturer of modern cars in Ukraine. Up to 1991 annual growth was in the range of 14 - 15 per cent and the capacity in 1993 was 300,000 cars a year.

Table 5.2 Car production in Avtozaz, 1991 - 1996

1991	1992	1993	1994	1995	1996
156,000	135,000	140,000	94,000	57,000	7,000

Source: Business Central Europe, March 1997

In 1992 the Ukrainian government was still ambitious and optimistic and saw a brilliant future for the national car industry. A national car manufacturing plan was drawn up, a lot of money was channelled to Avtozaz and, in 1992, a new line was installed equipped with Western machinery.[24] However, in 1996 only 7,000 cars were produced and by mid-1997 the very survival of the factory was in question. From early December 1996 production stopped; by January 1998, the factory was still closed. Personnel had been sent home on unpaid leave.

Decline of production was delayed until relatively late, in 1993, due to the fact that many people were on waiting lists and there was still a shortage of cars. In August 1993 there were plans to expand production of cars up to 550,000 by the year 2000.

At the same time the import of cars increased tremendously. In 1994, Ukraine imported 160,000 cars, during the first nine months of 1995 200,000. On only 15 per cent of these cars was any import tax paid. From 1 January 1996 import tariffs for cars from the 'far abroad' have been raised sharply, in order to protect Avtozaz.

The enterprise directors blamed external factors for the decline, mentioning high taxes as a reason. However, government and parliament repeatedly helped Avtozaz. For example, the parliament decided in November 1995 that Avtozaz did not have to pay taxes for 1994. In May 1996 there was the slashing of import duties.

Apart from high taxes, supplies from Russia have been mentioned as a major problem. Eighty per cent of car parts, in value terms, came from Russia. Many of these parts were too expensive and could be obtained cheaper from Central and Western Europe.[25] Often, Avtozaz stuck to Russian suppliers because they accepted Avtozaz cars in return for payment. Another problem was that some Russian suppliers came to see Avtozaz as a competitor and stopped deliveries.[26]

The gradual decline of supplies, that had started already during the Perestroika years negatively affected the quality of the cars produced by Avtozaz, because the substitute supplies, or spare parts, were often of poorer quality, especially that of the engine delivered by the factory in Melitopol.[27]

Also, supplies became more expensive. In early 1993 production costs for a car were 3000 dollars. Later that year production costs increased to 3,700 dollars and by August 1996 it amounted to 4800 dollars.

A factor in rising costs was the very high material costs and intensive energy use of production. As costs of energy and raw materials increased after independence, this was reflected in production costs.

The developing financial crisis of Avtozaz made the factory a bad client for its suppliers, who often were not paid. Suppliers began to ask payment in advance. Barter trade was not important as it became too expensive with the introduction of 20 percent value added tax on barter transactions. Whereas in Soviet times disruption in production due to non-delivery of supplies never happened, during transition this occurred more frequently.

People in the street, the potential consumers, complain about the bad quality of the Tavria, the car currently produced. The Tavria is notorious for continuously breaking down. It is relatively much cheaper to buy a second-hand Western car rather than buy, for the same amount of money, a Tavria.

The core problem of Avtozaz has never been mentioned in the Ukrainian press: the way production was organised, for example, quality control. Although a quality control system existed on paper, it did not function in practice. For example, it often happened that parts of the car were not available. In Western car factories, production would have stopped immediately. Not in Zaporizhzhya. There production continued and workers were asked to write down what elements of the car were missing. However, workers often forgot to do this. The result was that cars were delivered that were missing elements, often quite essential ones. A worker in Avtozaz told how he was asked to drive an approved car to the parking place in order to be shipped. After having switched the motor on, he found that the wheel was not fixed and it came away in his hand.

In Zaporizhzhya often young women of 18 to 20 years worked on the assembly line. They were not strong enough to perform some of the required tasks with the result of bad performance. Employees told how, usually, other employees exhibited a lack of responsibility. They were not at all interested in good performance. The only thing that counted was quantity, not quality.

A big problem in the factory was alcoholism. According to estimates of several informers from within the factory (no hard data exist on alcoholism which has attained epidemic proportions in Zaporizhzhya), most male workers drank in the workplace.[28] It is obvious that this had a very negative impact upon work performance. A journalist from the *Wall Street Journal* hinted at this low labour productivity when writing in 1989 that 'for every worker on the line, there are several who sit on a wooden bench nearby, watching, chatting and smoking cigarettes. Behind the facade of modern production, quite primitive production methods prevailed.

Remarkably for Avtozaz, since 1993, when the production decline began, there was no organisational restructuring.[29] No personnel were dismissed - the total amount of personnel was at the end of 1995 28,855 persons, significantly more compared to 1990, producing 60,000 cars. For comparison, Nissan car factory in Sunderland, UK, had a production of

216,800 cars with 3,500 workers in 1992.[30] No organisational changes have been introduced in order to enhance quality of production.

Up to early 1996, there was a big problem with spare parts as they disappeared to the black market sphere. Only since then, when production of cars was stopped, was everything being done, according to the enterprise director, to satisfy the demand for spare parts.

Before 1996, the marketing of cars in the former Soviet Union had been done through in an informal manner and, less importantly, through car centres (25 in Ukraine and 68 in Russia). Since then every buyer had the same rights and paid the same price.[31]

In mid-1996, after the former director has been dismissed and the factory had lain idle for half a year, the enterprise leadership started de-coupling the cultural sphere and the hospital and agricultural sector (4 kolkhozes) from the car factory and making the technical service independent. Salary of factory workers halved.

The enterprise management of Avtozaz claimed that relatively modern equipment, bought in Japan and Western Europe, was in place. The Ukrainian press wrote that Avtozaz is a very modern factory.[32] However, Coopers and Lybrand in 1993 found the technological level of equipment mediocre. They concluded that in the long run the factory had no future. Investment funds have been channelled to a new assembly line with Western equipment was installed in 1992. The rest of the factory is completely outdated. Even the new production line is not modern as it is not fully automated but handled manually.

Negotiations have taken place since 1994 with Daewoo, Peugeot, Rover and General Motors. Due to an unrealistic assessment about the value of Avtozaz on the part of the Ukrainian government, erroneous negotiation strategy and general bad conditions for foreign direct investment in Ukraine, it was three years before agreement could be reached.

In mid-September 1997, the Ukrainian government announced that Daewoo, the South Korean car manufacturer, would invest 1.3 billion dollars up to 2003 in its joint venture with Avtozaz. That is more than the total accumulated foreign direct investment in Ukraine as a whole by mid-1997. According to the Financial Times (17 September 1997), the company plans to develop a new engine and update the Tavria. General Motors plans to sign a separate deal with Daewoo-Avtozaz to build 25,000 units a year. Daewoo is believed to have gained the edge over General Motors in negotiations with the Ukrainian government by promising to invest in a range of manufacturing industries.

However, only March 1998 a contract has been signed. The problem was that Avotzaz promised to prepare assembly lines for the production of five models by end 1997. When a Daewoo team came to Zaporizhzhya to inspect progress, they noticed that nothing had been done.

Nowadays, only 62 out of 1000 Ukrainian citizens has a car while the corresponding figure for Germany is 490 and for Italy 425, a clear indicator of the growth potential of the Ukrainian market.

Motor Sitch

This company manufactures engines for aircraft, mainly for the military. With the collapse of the Soviet Union and therewith the collapse of its military industrial complex, the factory lost its major market. The civil aviation division also went through a crisis parallel with the general economic crisis. Few new planes have been ordered. According to the Zaporizhzhya Statistical Office, production decline of Motor Sitch is twice as much as for Zaporizhzhya industry in general.

It is mainly the replacement of old engines and repairwork that production levels have not fallen more steeply. The question of survival of this factory has been posed in the press.[33] The problem with Soviet engines was, among other things, their high energy consumption.[34] Also the image of low technology hampers advance in export markets.

Whereas many other aircraft manufacturers in Central and Eastern Europe have sought strategic alliances with world leaders in aviation industry, Motor Sitch has not done so, in part because the industry is considered a strategic one. However, it is difficult to imagine future competitiveness without linking up with world leaders.

In 1995 there were negotiations with BMW/Rolls Royce in order to develop the joint production of an aircraft engine. In the negotiations about the 100-million-dollar project the technical design was not a problem. The main problems concerned marketing aspects and, above all, quality control. The directors of Motor Sitch also refused to speak about long-term strategy. In the meantime, BMW/Rolls Royce has found a partner in Russia.

Another problem for Motor Sitch is brain drain. Highly qualified engineers find jobs elsewhere in town or in the Russian aviation industry, where they are better paid.

In contrast to the drastic decline in mainline production, sideline production has developed enormously. The product range varies from generators to garden equipment and baby carriages.[35]

Though the export level is very low related to the size of the factory, Motor Sitch is an interesting potential partner for foreign investors. Equipment is quite modern and work organisation better than many other industrial enterprises, as it used to be a core factory within the military industrial complex. Nowadays, there is the joint production of a van engine, in co-operation with IVECO, a subsidiary of FIAT, for IVECO-Kraz, that will produce approximately 4000 small vans annually for the Ukrainian market.[36]

Organisational restructuring in large enterprises

For each of the eight largest enterprises, organisational restructuring hardly took place, apart from the dismissal of personnel in the form of sending on unpaid leave. According to the Zaporizhzhya Statistical Office, in the period 1991 - 1995 employment of the seven largest enterprises even increased from 90,122 to 93,984.

These figures do not give an indication for actual employment. For example, Zaporozhstal actually employed by the end of 1995 only about 3000 workers. However, the people listed as being employed by Zaporozhstal still make use of some services of Zaporozhstal, like housing.

There are significant differences with respect to adjustment. While Transformerzavod introduced new products and has devoted greater attention to marketing, in Avtozaz very little has changed. This difference is also related to the completely different character of the production process, Avtozaz mass producing one product, Transformerzavod concentrating on individual production.

Ferrosplavzavod changed somewhat more than Zaporozhstal, the former having introduced some new equipment. Probably this has much to do with differences in management.

Generally, there were few incentives for management to change. Their salaries are high and guaranteed, irrespective of performance. [37]

For all big enterprises the word 'restructuring' has meant installing new machinery and equipment. The production process is conceived as a purely technical process, for which only engineers can be experts. This reflects the Soviet view towards production. In Soviet times, almost no attention has been paid to management, marketing, cost accounting, quality control and the organisation of production. This Soviet view is not only currently predominant among the management of big enterprises, but in the whole political and economic elite of Zaporizhzhya.

In newspaper articles and interviews, problems of enterprises were always analysed in terms of external problems: taxes, lack of demand and so on. The solution for the problems was always money from external sources.

It is telling, that by 1997, six years after the proclaimed changeover to a market economy, none of the big enterprises knows the real cost price of their products, nor do they know how much the social sphere of their enterprise costs - no one has introduced an elementary modern system of cost accounting.

Although prospects for the analysed enterprises may be different, for each of them survival in the circumstances of the market economy may be unlikely, with the possible exceptions of Dneprospetsstal and Ferrosplavzavod.

Various industrial sectors

The agro-industrial complex

The food processing industry in Zaporizhzhya province accounted in 1995 for 8.5 per cent of total industrial production, and for 24 per cent of total personnel.[38]

It is especially in the food processing sector that import competition is severe. The market is flooded with food products from Western and Central Europe. In the present circumstances, i.e. high inflation, Mafia, high taxes and lack of investment, it is quite difficult to be competitive against Western enterprises. If the economy becomes stabilised and law governed, ample opportunities exist in this sector. With relatively small investments, great improvements in product quality and productivity can be achieved. Some factories, like the Melitopol meat enterprise, provide examples how to produce well in current difficult circumstances.[39]

Often, food processing enterprises prefer inputs from abroad as they are of better quality. For example, ZTL, a juice-producing factory, shifted from Ukrainian supplies of concentrate, with a shelf-life of only one month, to concentrates from Hungary and Israel, that lasted respectively one year and half a year.

ZTL now tries to produce eggs and egg flour in co-operation with a chicken farm in Hungary. They will buy from Hungary chickens and chicken food and will restart a chicken farm that has stopped production earlier because it did not have enough money to buy food for the chickens.

The electronic industry

About 50,000 persons were employed in this sector in 1992, among them 12,500 scientific workers.[40] The enterprises in this sector were often working for the military and mostly subordinated to ministries in Moscow. Production felt steeply in this sector. The greatest problems were lack of spare parts, loss of traditional markets and loss by non-payment of deliveries to clients. Detailed figures can not be given as this sector has not been classified separately in the statistics.

The machine-building industry

In terms of employment this is the most important sector in Zaporizhzhya province. Fifty-five per cent of industrial workers were employed in this sector in 1995. Transformerzavod, Motor Sitch and Avtozaz are included in this sector. There are many smaller enterprises in this sector, with, in many cases, close relationship to the steel industry in Zaporizhzhya.

According to inside information and circumstantial evidence, this sector suffered relatively much in recent years, as most enterprises stopped investing in new tools or equipment and as the markets of the countries of the former Soviet Union collapsed. Enterprises in this branch are usually not able to export to the 'far abroad'. A large part of this industry previously used to produce for the military.

One of the better performing factories is Zaporozhavtomatika, producing equipment for metallurgical enterprises.

The chemical industry

This industry did relatively well in recent years, compared to other industries. Production decline has only been 15 per cent in the period 1990 - 1995 while the industry as a whole declined by 34 per cent. This branch has, however, very limited importance for Zaporizhzhya. It contributed only 0.9 per cent to total industrial production in the region.[41]

An important and successful enterprise in this branch is Kremnipolimer, that used to be part of Magnesium and Titanium Enterprise.

The consumer goods industry

Unlike many had expected at the early 1990s, the consumer goods industry faced the largest decline, in Zaporizhzhya and in Ukraine at large (see Appendix 2). For example, in Zaporizhzhya, the production of clothing declined in the period 1992 -1996 by 89 per cent, that of underclothes by 97 per cent.[42]

This sharp decline in the production of consumer goods is related to the sharp drop in demand in Ukraine and the low quality of consumer goods produced in Ukraine. The larger market share has taken over by foreign, mainly Western competitors.

In Zaporizhzhya province, there are few textile and clothing factories. The factories that work for the domestic market have closed or hardly function. The textile factory Vepes, with 300 employees, producing mainly overalls for local enterprises, had increasingly to rely on sideline activities to keep the enterprise afloat. About six years ago there were difficulties in getting supplies, related to the disarray caused by the dissolution of the Soviet Union. Nowadays the main problem is to find money to pay for supplies. Most of the cotton used (95 per cent) comes from Russia where it is also processed into yarn (this used to be done in Kharkiv).

The few clothing factories that mainly produce for export are not integrated into the local economy and do not even know each other. We interviewed managers from Kora (60 employees) and Selena (500 employees) each of which has Western machinery and textile raw materials. Designs come partly from the West (in both cases about half their designs are from the Western partner, the other half are their own designs). All supplies come from the West as Ukrainian suppliers are considered unreliable and of low quality. In the case of Kora there is a joint venture with a German partner (formed in 1994, Neckermann). One year ago, Kora still had a significant part of production for the domestic market. Nowadays almost 100 per cent of its production is for export.

Organisational change

In the section about Avtozaz, it has been explained how organisation of the workforce did not change during transition, although the primitive organisation of labour is a main cause for the lack of quality. This situation is typical for big industrial enterprises. Generally, the labour morale and labour productivity are very low.

Also in the newly privatised firms it seems that not much organisational change has occurred, probably related to a lack of marketisation of the economic environment. The conclusion of a recent analysis of privatisation and industrial restructuring in Ukraine may be true for Zaporizhzhya as well. The report concluded:

> It appears that managers and employees have temporarily achieved a modus vivendi: employees are putting pressure on managers who maintain the level of employment and income, while managers are considering only external factors (market conditions and relations with trade partners) as the major constraints on the process of decision makers.[43]

Management skills are very low. Usually, the managers had an engineering education and do not have any notion of modern production organisation. Typical are the many levels in the enterprise hierarchy. A general characteristic of the Zaporizhzhya industrial enterprise, compared with Western industrial enterprises, is the high share of administrative personnel.

There is usually little attention given to quality control and marketing. A modern accounting system is usually missing, with the result that there is no evaluation of production costs. It is noticeable that trade unions hardly play a role in corporate governance.

Generally, there is lack of marketing and communication skills. With regard to communication skills, generally, firms are not able to write down in clear terms what they want from outsiders. It is related to the lack of writing culture in Soviet times. Unlike Western firms, enterprises in Ukraine seldom had to communicate in written form with clients, the suppliers, the ministries or their own personnel. In Soviet times as well as nowadays, commitments in written form might have turned against you. Communication mostly has been in oral form. In the economy of shortage the firm had no lack of customers, and supplies could be arranged in negotiations with the ministries and with 'horizontal', informal deals with other firms; as a result, no 'civilised' business culture could develop.

It is striking to see how much difficulty industrial enterprises in Zaporizhzhya have, up to the larger ones, in making a good business plan or making a good presentation for potential investors.

Conclusion

The prospects for the large industrial enterprises are gloomy. Without subsidies, that are mostly hidden, most of them will not be able to survive. For many years, almost nothing has been invested and equipment is outdated. Industrial Zaporizhzhya has become a big rust belt that is difficult to regenerate. Organisational change has barely taken place. New industrial enterprises hardly can develop as they are squeezed by high taxes and bureaucratic regulations. The privatisation process is proceeding very slowly and does not have an impact upon industrial production as the general environment of industrial firms is little influenced by the philosophy of the market economy.

Notes

1. *Delovaya Ukraina*, 15 November 1995, pp. 1, 2.
2. For example, the director of Transformerzavod complained in an interview (*Telenedelja*, 26 February. - 3 March 1996) that 60,000 people are living in the residential district of Transformerzavod, many of them not employees of Transformerzavod. and some enterprises are settled in this quarter of town. However, many of these tenants and enterprises have accumulated large debts with Transformerzavod.
3. This typical corporate culture explains the fact that, relatively, so few strikes have occurred during transition. Strikes were mainly in branches where the corporate culture differed significantly from the one that has been described here. An example is mining. See Crowley, 1994.
4. *Nash Gorod*, 29 December 1992, pp. 1, 2.
5. *Industrialnoje Zaporizhzhya*. Mrs Efimenko, responsible for economic affairs within the province administration claims that nowadays there are no direct subsidies for the steel industry. They may sell relatively cheaply due to the provision of cheap inputs, like energy, through special barter deals, very low or no amortisation rates and the fact that very little is spent for environmental protection. Moreover, in the last years they could profit from the use of cheaply bought inputs, these were bought and stored at times that prices of these inputs were still very low. Subsidies may also be in the form of non-payment of deliveries. According to Dolgorudov (1995), Zaporozhstal's debt was in 1994 132 per cent of its annual turnover (p.40).
6. Egorov, 1996.

7. An article in the weekly *Bisnes* (4 February 1997) argued how, despite growth in 1996, ferrous metallurgy in Donetsk has become less profitable. The exchange rate policy of the government contributed to this.
8. *Nash Gorod*, 29 May 1996.
9. Percentages for Russia are for 1995 14 per cent, for 1994 42 per cent and for 1993 16 per cent. Zaporizke 1996b.
10. See van Zon, H. 1996.
11. Zaporizhzhya Statistical Office.
12. Zaporizhzhya Statistical Office.
13. Most of the information about this enterprise has been given by Professor Falkevich, who has worked many years for this enterprise.
14. Coopers and Lybrand, 1993.
15. *Industralnoje Zaporizhzhya*, 1 April 1994, p. 2.
16. Zaporizke, 1996c. p. 104.
17. This institute has recently designed a magnesium factory for Israel.
18. *Nash Gorod*, 11 June 1993, p. 2.
19. Coopers and Lybrand, 1993.
20. Zaporizhzhya Statistical Office. However, in an interview with Reuters (1 March 1994), the director of Aluminium Enterprise declared that all output, approximately. 120,000 tonnes a year, was fully absorbed by the Russian Federation. In this case, probably the statistical office is right and not the director.
21. Coopers and Lybrand, 1993, p. 10.
22. Coopers and Lybrand, 1993, p. 6.
23. In March 1993, the average wage in Aluminium Enterprise was, according to the exchange rate at that time, 9.5 - 12 dollars a month. In December 1995, the average wage in light metallurgy was 146 dollars, given a dollar-karbonavets exchange rate of 1:187,000. With most Western competitors, workers have to pay from their salary for services that workers in Aluminium Enterprise get free as part of the social sphere of the enterprise. If we include the social sphere of the enterprise in the wages of production workers, by assessing the cost of this social sphere per production worker, their wages become much higher. In 1993, Coopers and Lybrand assumed that to get the real wage of production workers, that is the costs for the social sphere included in their wage, the official average wage of the average production worker should be multiplied by a factor of 4.3. For the end of 1995, this means that the real average wage of production workers, assuming that the social sphere has had the same weight as early 1993, would be in the range of 628 dollars. Since the end of 1995, the wage in dollar terms increased as inflation remained substantial while the national currency revalued against the dollar!
24. However, investments were focused at the assemblyline of the Tavria. The result was that major new bottlenecks arose. The capacity of the engine factory in Melitopol was just enough to produce half of the engines needed in Avtozaz. The remaining funds, left after the installation of the new line, were not even enough

to pay for petrol to test new cars, according to *Zerkalo Nedeli* (1 March 1997). According to *Business Central Europe* (March 1997), it took Avtozaz 10 years (1982 - 1992) to install an Italian-equipped assembly plant and paint shop. The Western machinery bought in Soviet times, often remained, up to today, unpacked as the workers did not know what to do with it. Also, the new assembly line did not function well as it had not been well installed.

25. Cold-rolled steel is supplied by Russia, for 629 dollars per tonne. But in Slovakia this costs 470 dollars, The ignition costs 23 dollars in Russia, but in Western Europe 20 dollars. The induction coil costs in Russia 37 dollars, but in Poland only 17 dollars (information obtained by enterprise visit).
26. *Delovoj Novosti*, 10 January 1995.
27. *Bisnes*, 3 September 1996.
28. This estimate is based on interviews with several employees of Avtozaz. This estimate is confirmed by accounts of alcoholism in other big enterprises. Only in the firms that were incorporated in the military complex, was the alcohol problem under better control.
29. The only substantial measure taken was to fire, in 1993, all workers that have attained the pension age. This measure caused widespread indignation.
30. Lyndon Dods, p. 117. According to the *Economist* (16 November 1996), Nissan produces 58 cars per employee per year (Opel Eisenach 72). If Zaporizhzhya workers had the same productivity as Nissan, with 20,000 workers Avtozaz should produce 1,160,000 cars per year.
31. *Bisnes*, 3 September 1996, p. 23.
32. For example, the all-Ukrainian *Bisnes* (3 September 1996) claimed that 'Avtozaz has the most modern assembly in Europe, with machinery installed in 1992.' In their information about Avtozaz, journalists solely rely on information given by the enterprise management, often gives false information.
33. *Industrialnoje Zaporizhzhya*, 22 July 1995, p. 2.
34. That was the reason that already in the early 1980s the Hungarians, and soon other East European companies, began to buy Western aircraft. Soviet aircraft was far too expensive in exploitation.
35. *Industrialnoje Zaporizhzhya*, 20 September 1994, p. 2.
36. Reuters, 27 December 1995.
37. For example, the salary of the director of Motor Sitch amounted September 1996 to 3000 dollars per month, 1996, while employees of his firm did not receive their salary for four months.
38. Zaporizke 1996a, p. 28.
39. This factory closely co-operates with an Austrian firm.
40. Coopers and Lybrand, 1993, p. 14.
41. Zaporizke 1996b, p. 8.
42. Zaporizke, 1997b.
43. Frausum et al., p. 20.

Zaporizhzhya: the dam in river Dnepr

The bazaar near October Square

Zaporizhzhya: industrial district

Zaporizhzhya: residential area

6 The Transformation of the Countryside

The divide between countryside and towns

About 25 - 30 per cent of the population of Zaporizhzhya lives in the countryside, that is in settlements smaller than 50,000 inhabitants. They are predominantly Ukrainian speaking. Also, some ethnic minorities, like Bulgarians, Gypsies and Greeks, live in the countryside.

The smaller settlements are characterised by collective agricultural enterprises with their barns and places where small-scale food processing takes place. The smaller settlements usually look abandoned and public services are scarce. Asphalt roads are rare. Living conditions in the countryside are very poor as they have little access to services that are common for towns: hospitals, good schools, cultural facilities, etc. There are few shops - many settlements do not have shops at all. There are no recreational facilities in small settlements and there are no pubs although alcoholism is epidemic. People in small settlements regularly die from diseases that could be easily treated, due to the absence of adequate medical care. Travelling by train and bus to towns has become much more expensive, as public transport has deteriorated enormously.

It is common that drinking water comes from wells, not purified. Even in the outskirts of Zaporizhzhya many people have to get drinking water from wells. In many cases drinking water is brought in vans from the towns.

Most houses in the countryside do not have gas and must pay the full price for heating, including the heating of water, which has become quite expensive. A lot of houses in smaller settlements do not even have electricity.

Since the mid 1980s the process of the gradual closing of the welfare gap between towns and the countryside, ongoing since the reign of Khrushchev, has been reversed and the gap between living conditions in the countryside and town has widened again. Average income in the countryside, that always has been far below average, dropped faster than the incomes of town inhabitants. Of course, all inhabitants of the countryside have access to private gardens, the products of which they can sell on the market. On the other hand they miss access to other sources of income.

Traditionally, young and talented people tend to leave for the towns. Although this is a phenomenon one can see everywhere in the world, this has been more pronounced in the former Soviet Union, given the extremely bad conditions in the countryside. The countryside has an ageing population and traditional social pathologies, such as alcoholism, are more widespread.

In many ways, relations between towns and countryside have been severed. Townspeople who own gardens in the countryside, cannot afford to go there anymore due to the inability to pay for transport costs, unless they are pensioners who can travel free.

Increasingly, people in towns try to profit from their connections in the countryside by organising trade in food products. Nevertheless, in most cases kolkhozes have a conservative leadership that prevents development. Generally, the criminalisation of power constitutes a formidable obstacle for the development of the countryside.

Collective and private farms

Most agricultural land is still under cultivation by collective farms, i.e. the kolkhozes. In theory, they were 'denationalised' by July 1996 and the land is privately owned by the farmers. In practice, kolkhozes began to distribute land to its members very slowly. By mid-1997, about half of the land had been distributed among farmers. Part of the land is leased to non-farmers.

When Ukraine became independent, most experts pointed to agriculture as one of the country's main assets, due to its fertile soils.[1] Nowadays, agriculture is in deep crisis and for many years practically nothing has been invested. Harvests gradually declined due to degradation of soils and organisational and financial problems of the kolkhozes. In the period 1990 - 1996 agricultural production in Zaporizhzhya province decreased by 52.5 per cent in value terms, that of Ukraine by 40.6 per cent.

Grain production in Zaporizhzhya province decreased from 2454 thousand tonnes in 1992 to 874 thousand tonnes in 1996.[2] It means that grain production in what used to be the bread basket of the former Soviet Union, dropped by almost two-thirds in a time span of four years. Formerly there was a harvest of up to 3.5 tonnes of grain per hectare. It is now 1.3 tonnes.[3] Part of the grain is sold to the state that pays a price far below the world market price. In 1996 the state paid the farmers 85 dollars per tonne when the world market price was 200 dollars per tonne. The difference from the world market price went to corrupt officials.[4]

The quality of grains produced is generally very low. For the production of high-quality bread - imported grain is used. The low quality is related to the lack of care for crops. Lack of money over many years deprived kolkhozes of the means to grow high-quality grains.

For example, in Orechov, kolkhozes used to have 40 to 50 tractors. However, due to lack of investments nowadays, only 3 to 4 tractors per kolkhoze are functioning.[5] In one malfunction, spare parts are not available as the tractor factory in Kharkiv cannot provide spare parts anymore.

By mid-1997 the price of milk in shops is more than seven times higher than the price kolkhozes get for milk. It points to the general problem that a large part of the price the consumer pays for agricultural products is for trade, processing and the Mafia.

For collective agricultural enterprises, it has become more difficult to sell their products in towns because the traditional system of state wholesale suppliers broke down. Although the system of state orders still exist, state prices are so low that collective enterprises try to circumvent the state wherever possible. However, successfully functioning wholesale markets have not replaced the system of state orders and distribution. It has been replaced by Mafiosi structures that are very unfavourable for agricultural enterprises. Furthermore, there is the system of barter exchanges with big enterprises. Every sixth tonne of fuel earmarked for big enterprises in Zaporizhzhya is destined for kolkhozes in barter deals.[6]

The negotiating position of agricultural enterprises have worsened enormously under transition resulting in declining incomes. It is telling that the employees of a dairy firm, producing milk, get a salary that is 2.5 times higher compared to that of the farmers.

Most kolkhozes have not invested anymore in equipment since the early 1980s. Due to lack of orders the whole service infrastructure for agricultural enterprises has broken down. Often, these services are located in the countryside. Also, the farm equipment industry does not produce anymore. For example, the national tractor industry, located in Kharkiv, has collapsed due to lack of demand. A great problem for kolkhozes has been that, during the 1990s, prices for agricultural products increased at a lower rate than the non-agricultural goods and the services kolkhozes used to buy.

Generally, agriculture suffers from mismanagement, low productivity (yields are 30 - 50 per cent lower than in Western Europe, pig and milk productivity are 200 per cent lower), lack of inputs, absence of appropriate trading infrastructure, lack of economic understanding and knowledge, obsolete equipment and high production costs.

It is obvious that the economic system does not stimulate agricultural production. Farmers are shifting their energy more to cultivating their private gardens which means that farming becomes more primitive.

The kolkhozes have little money, often even the very low kolkhoze salaries of 25 - 30 dollars a month cannot be paid. The average kolkhoze has a debt of about 6000 dollars, mainly due to the inability to pay for energy and inputs. Much trade is now on barter basis. Agricultural workers can only survive by selling products from private plots in the bazaar. The following figures are telling: 3 per cent of the surface of cultivated land in Ukraine consist of private gardens, but these private plots provide about 65 per cent of produced vegetables, 96 per cent of potatoes, 70 per cent of fruits and 53 per cent of meat.[7]

Also, the prices on the black market are rather high, in part to compensate for low kolchoze salaries. One egg in the bazaar costs about 0,15 cents, not much less compared to eggs in Western Europe. Generally, prices for food products are extremely high compared to the average salary in Ukraine.

Few collective farmers want to start a private farm, for many reasons. First of all, one has to pay for the land. Moreover, farmers usually do not have money. To run a private farm, one has to buy equipment. Again, there is usually no money. Then there is the problem of know-how: most farmers do not possess the knowledge to start a farm.

Nevertheless private farms are gradually spreading. According to Ukrainian authorities, approximately half of agricultural production is now on private plots. Private farmers are mainly in Western Ukraine, less so in Eastern Ukraine.

The food industry

There is a kind of deadlock situation in the countryside as there are apparently no mechanisms that may trigger a revival of agricultural production. With normally functioning markets, the agricultural and food-processing sectors would be one of the most promising: people need to eat and a lot of food products that are now imported can also be produced in Ukraine. At Zaporizhzhya markets, Dutch butter and cheese is sold, produced by farmers and firms that produce at the other end of Europe, where labour costs are much higher. However, agricultural enterprises in Zaporizhzhya are squeezed by the state and Mafiosi commercial structures that prevent profitable agricultural enterprises from developing.

Lack of money has prevented kolkhozes from investing, with the result that suppliers of agriculture equipment have also fallen in deep crisis.[8]

According to French specialists working for the TACIS sunflower project in Zaporizhzhya, the few big firms that are active in the trading and processing of sunflower oil are connected with Mafia groupings. These firms earn a lot with these activities while the kolkhozes get little money. In exchange for sunflowers, the kolkhozes get products. The strategy of the sunflower project is to induce kolkhozes to form co-operatives to improve their negotiating position.

Conclusion

With the disintegration of central planning, the welfare gap between town and countryside began to widen again. The absence of properly functioning markets and the disincentives for agricultural enterprises to produce caused a general impoverishment of the countryside and the collapse of agricultural production. Where private initiative gets more chance, development, nowadays quite uneven in the countryside, takes place. With good leadership and well-functioning markets, development prospects for the countryside are good.

Notes

1. However, soils are not as rich as is often assumed in the West. During the last decades erosion, the abundant use of pesticides and fertilizers and the use of too heavy machinery have depleted soil fertility.
2. Zaporizke, 1997a, p.49.
3. *Delovaya Ukraina*, 15 November 1995, p. 1, 2.
4. *International Herald Tribune*, 10 April 1997.
5. Information from M.I. Sotnikov, head of technical equipment division, Orechov.
6. *Delovaya Ukraina*, 15 November 1995, p. 1, 2.
7. *EIU Business Report Belarus/Ukraine*.
8. For example, there is a big tractor factory in Kharkiv, producing for the whole of the Ukraine. In 1995 6000 tractors were been produced but only 187 sold. (*Kyivskie Vedomosti*, 21 February 1996).

7 The Disintegration of Public Services

In Soviet times, a comprehensive network of public services developed of which every citizen could profit, often free of charge. The system included not only a developed educational and health care system but also pre-school facilities for children, school meals, a system of specialised schools, holiday resorts, cheap tickets for cultural events, very low tariffs for public transport, very low payment for rent and housing services and so on. The state could pay for it because it paid citizens lower salaries.

In the transition towards the market economy the system of public spending changed. In the scrabble for scarce resources, it was spending for all kind of public services that could be most easily cut.

This has led to a rapid deterioration of all kind of public services in Zaporizhzhya. In this chapter various public services in Zaporizhzhya town are described, with emphasis on the impact recent changes have had on the living conditions of the general population.

Health care

Soviet communism created an extended network of free health care services for the general population. Often, these services were provided by the individual enterprise and included not only polyclinics, but also a network of sanatoriums.

Up to the mid 1960s health services continued to expand and improve rapidly. Since that time health care was increasingly treated as a residual service, i.e. the financing of this sector came last, after all other expenditures have been met.[1] Traditionally, workers in health care are poorly paid, i.e. 70 - 75 per cent of the average salary.

In conditions of economic crisis the whole network of free medical services collapsed.[2] Also, enterprises started to dissociate their health care services. Sanatoriums closed, and all kinds of health care provisions were abolished. The number of people staying in sanatoriums and rest houses in Zaporizhzhya province decreased from 633,400 in 1990 to 291,900 in 1995.

Medical personnel was not only faced with a sharp cut in real salary but also with delay of salary payments: that amounted in early 1997 to about six months. By 1997, for medical doctors the salary was not enough to survive. Moreover, in 1997, 20 per cent of medical personnel has been dismissed, with the result of an increased workload for the remaining personnel.

This financial squeeze had the result that the practice of paying money for medical services spread rapidly. Nowadays, tariffs are set according to the assumed wealth of the patient.

Patients must pay for virtually everything. When going to hospital for an operation, the patient must supply sheets, bedclothes and food and pay for medicines and even bandages. The delivery of food in hospitals, of very bad quality, has been reduced to once a day.

Free medicines do not exist anymore. In the rare cases that they are given they are the most elementary and of low quality. Medicines are generally very expensive as all medicines are imported.

In the case of the very poor, sometimes free operations are done, but even then medicines must be paid for. This all means that without money, medical care is virtually non existent.

For the new rich, new private health establishments have been opned, but they offer bad services for high prices. For example, in 1996 the tariff for delivery service was more than 1000 dollars.

Having a child is nowadays very expensive in Zaporizhzhya as delivery in the hospital costs a lot of money. Abortion is also expensive. This is rather important for women as abortion is the main means of birth control.[3]

Famous health care institutions are on the verge of bankruptcy. There is for example the Centre for Rehabilitation of the Reproductive Functions of the Family where 230, mostly highly specialised, people help couples with fertility problems. Only five of such institutes exist in Ukraine and the Zaporizhzhya institute, with 100 beds, has an excellent reputation. Various new techniques have been developed here. Now, they are in a hopeless situation. In 1997, they had to cut the amount of beds by 15 - 20 per cent and they had to cut regularly the salaries of personnel. In 1997, the chief surgeon had to open a kiosk in order to earn some additional money to survive.

Education

Ukraine has inherited a developed and comprehensive educational system which starts at an early age. The three-tiered state education system remained in place, consisting of pre-school centres, combined primary-secondary schools for grades one through to eleven and higher education establishments.

Zaporizhzhya schools have gone through great changes since the late 1980s. In Perestroika times many teachers, especially those in history, literature and related subjects, made use of the new freedom and started to introduce new themes in the curriculum that were forbidden in previous times. The Zaporizhzhya institute devoted to furthering the professional level of teachers launched a lot of initiatives. There were also attempts to improve didactic methods and the more experienced teachers got the opportunity to experiment.

During the late 1980s and early 1990s new schools appeared in Zaporizhzhya such as gymnasiums and lyceums that build upon pre-Revolutionary experiences in Zaporizhzhya. In their first years these elite schools got additional state funding, the curriculum was deepened and widened to include new subjects and also didactic methods improved. Teachers at these schools received better payment. Directors had more scope of manoeuvre to experiment with curriculums and to select the best teachers. The directors of elite schools established relations with academies and universities and signed contracts about automatic admission of their graduates to these universities and academies.

The late 1980s was also a period in which many teachers became active in the political field. The teacher Sergei Gorbachev became member of the city Soviet and other teachers became local deputies on a programme of reform. By the early 1990s, they had become disillusioned and left politics. A new situation arose with independence: the former practice of sending excellent students to Moscow or St Petersburg, where by far the best education opportunities existed, was blocked.

From 1992 onwards, public authorities squeezed schools. Also, step by step, schools lost their previous freedoms. As a result of budget squeezes schools started to ask money from parents. Gradually a division in the educational system emerged: one education for the rich and another education for the poor. As a result of economic difficulties the very existence of elite schools is on the agenda.

Most schools operate in double shifts as there is a shortage of class rooms, though recently this problem has lessened somewhat as the birth rate has declined.

Most of the schools are very poor. In 1995 they abolished free lunches, which has been paid out of the municipal budget. They started to ask parents to pay for textbooks that were previously provided by the schools free of charge. Often schools try to charge the rich parents somewhat more to enable poorer children to have textbooks. By mid-1997 the schools often did not have the most elementary material: about 20 per cent of teachers have been dismissed with the result that the workingload of remaining teachers has become heavier.

Teachers were paid less and were faced with a delay in salary payments of about four months. Some teachers started asking money in exchange for good marks. This kind of corruption created a downward trend in the level of education.

The deterioration of the situation of schools is not only related to lack of money but also to mismanagement, and, sometimes, corruption, from the part of public authorities. Although senior civil servants boast in the news media about their low salaries, they are able to build luxury villas. When the money allocated for refurbishing a demolished building for the school Logos disappeared, the civil servant responsible for education bought a luxury four- room apartment and started to build a villa.

A positive change was the abolition of evening schools that used to give adult students diplomas without any obligations on the part of these students.

The 1990s constitutes for many institutes a period of name-changing: the pedagogical institute became the University of Zaporizhzhya, the famous Machine Building Institute became the Technical University and so on. Behind this facade was a gradual deterioration of the level of education due to economic difficulties. Higher education was faced with payment delays that were even longer compared to secondary education. Corruption became far more widespread than in secondary schools. It became usual in most institutes of higher education to buy good marks and common practice to graduate with the help of money.

A new development in higher education was the introduction of new economic disciplines like marketing, accounting and management studies. However, this was a cumbersome process as the newly appointed specialist often lack the necessary qualifications. For instance, the newly established faculty of management at the University of Zaporizhzhya was staffed by former linguists who took a four-week economics course from French consultants.

Science

One of the main victims of the economic crisis is science. Many of the independent research institutes in Zaporizhzhya have been closed.[4] In the period 1991 - 1994, the personnel of research institutes in Zaporizhzhya declined from 18,741 to 12,741.[5]

Although these research institutes often undertook tasks that were not really research tasks, like certification and standardisation, a large part of research capacity has been lost. The prevailing idea in the provincial administration is that market forces can decide what research activities are worth being saved. However, many highly qualified researchers and specialists try to move to other places as Zaporizhzhya cannot give them employment.

Generally, in Soviet times, there was an intensive exchange of scientists and teachers with other republics of the Soviet Union. This movement has meant a cross-fertilisation and enhanced considerably the level of science and teaching in Zaporizhzhya. With the breakdown of the former Soviet Union and the economic crisis, Zaporizhzhya became much more inward-looking and provincial, with adverse effects upon science and education.

The cultural sphere

Another public good that is in its development was to a large extent dependent on state support was that of various cultural activities. Whereas in the United States the sphere of culture is to a large extent dissociated from the state, in the former Soviet Union culture was a sphere almost totally occupied and furthered by the state. Since the economic crisis started this situation has worked out the most unfavourably for the cultural sphere.

Already in Soviet times, those choosing a career in the arts or the creation of knowledge opted for a career with, in most cases, no financial rewards. The creative intelligentsia in the former Soviet Union was predisposed to marginality.

Zaporizhzhya was traditionally a town with shallow cultural traditions and the local authorities did little to keep talented artists in town.

Traditionally, many of the best artists and scientists moved to other towns, especially Kyiv, Moscow and Leningrad. With the economic crisis that developed after the proclamation of independence of Ukraine, this outward movement increased. Those who stayed in Zaporizhzhya were in most cases fully marginalised and impoverished.

Among the famous artists who left Zaporizhzhya were the actors Victor Koshel and Anatoly Jashchenko, the violonist Maxim Panfilo, the theatre commentator Gaydabura and the accordionist Jan Tabachnik. Many talented artists suffered from alcoholism. The famous trumpetist L.M. was found dead in his apartment where his corpse was lay for many days, surrounded by empty bottles. The same was the fate of several good poets. The talented photographer J.S., who has had several exhibitions abroad, worked for many years in a small basement without any daylight. Recently all his negatives were destroyed as a result of flooding. For many years he has had few orders and lives in deep poverty. The excellent violinist B., first violin in the Philharmonic Orchestra of Zaporizhzhya has become a teacher who now earns such a small salary that he must choose between buying bread and buying medicines to cure his cancer. Many other examples can be given of talented artists that have come to live in deep poverty.

Many cultural establishments have been closed. In Soviet times there were fourteen music schools in Zaporizhzhya where children received special musical education from age 6 to 18. In those times parents had to pay additional money to let their children study at these schools. With the economic crisis most parents could no longer afford the needed school fees and most music schools closed. The surviving schools became very small and their educational level declined. Former music school teachers became teachers in normal schools and the most fortunate relied solely on private lessons.

Professional musicians, with a classical education, now often have to play in restaurants. The musicians of the Philharmonic Orchestra often have second, third or even fourth jobs to survive. They often play popular music at the parties of the new rich. In these difficult circumstances most professional musicians see their professional level decline.

Many cultural establishments closed their doors or changed their function. Oktjabrskye cultural palace transformed part of the palace into a centre with luxury shops, bar, massage centre and hair salon for the new rich. Another big cultural palace became a noisy cafe-restaurant where the new rich organise their parties. The Kirov cultural palace created two fashionable halls for parties. The sporting complex Orbita was transformed into a centre for the new rich with a sauna and shops. This is the general picture for cultural and sport centres in Zaporizhzhya. Amateur cultural life, that was mainly based in cultural centres, suffered enormously under the new circumstances.

Publishing is an important cultural activity. Nowadays it is very difficult to publish books. State support for publishing books has disappeared and the public cannot afford to buy books. Until 1995 there was in Zaporizhzhya still a thriving book market. Since then this market collapsed and by mid-1997 there was not one good bookshop left in Zaporizhzhya. Also the central system of ordering books has collapsed so that it is not even possible to order books. Bookselling is not profitable anymore. It is noticeable that among the many new fashionable shops there is not one bookshop reflecting the low cultural level of the new rich.

For authors in Zaporizhzhya it has become much more difficult to publish in Russia and other republics of the former Soviet Union. Exhibitions in these republics have also become more difficult. The collapse of the former Soviet Union and East European communism in general has contributed to the provincialisation of cultural life in Zaporizhzhya.

The cultural programme became very meagre as its traditional audience has become impoverished. The three theatres in town and the only concert hall have drastically reduced the number of performances. The programme of cultural activities in Zaporizhzhya, with 900,000 inhabitants, is now comparable with an average town of 50,000 - 100,000 inhabitants in Western Europe.

This decline in cultural activities is shown in statistics. Whereas there were in 1990 25 theatre visits per 100 inhabitants of Zaporizhzhya province, in 1995 this has declined to 11; in 1990 there were 33 concert visits per 100 inhabitants, in 1995 this has declined to 19.[6] The cinema is for the masses and here the decline in visits is more dramatic. Whereas there were in 1990 twelve films shown per one inhabitant, in 1994 this declined to one film and in 1995 to zero. The number of cinema visits decreased from 24.2 million in 1990 to 0.7 million in 1995. Many cinemas in Zaporizhzhya have been closed.

Care for pensioners, the disabled and orphans

Pensioners

Old people suffered tremendously under transition to a new social and economic system. First of all the purchasing power of pensions dropped drastically. By mid-1997, the average monthly pension (50 - 70 hrivna, i.e. 25 - 35 dollars) was for many pensioners just enough to pay one-third of their gas bill. It means that pensioners cannot survive on just their pension and are totally dependent on their families. This new situation has had a very negative impact on relations between pensioners and their children as most of these children do not have enough money to support their parents. Traditionally, families lived very closely together. With increasing financial difficulties, family relations came under strain. Under a new law, the state can forbid people, i.e. often pensioners, to sell their property in case they have debts. It means that most pensioners cannot hand over their house to their children as most pensioners have debts.

Often, there is no money to be buried in a normal way. Regularly, old people are buried without a coffin, or, children must leave their dead parents for a longer time in the morgue until they have collected enough money for a normal funeral. A coffin costs 80 hrivna, while the pension sometimes is 35 hrivna. Many people do not have 80 hrivna in cash. It was a tradition in Zaporizhzhya to collect money in the neighbourhood when someone died. One used to give a symbolic amount. Nowadays, relatives often beg their neighbours for more money in order to enable a funeral to take place. It has been tradition in Zaporizhzhya to hire an small orchestra for a funeral. Nowadays, very few people can afford that. Moreover, the funeral service is very corrupted. Usually, the funeral directors propose that the relatives bury the day following the death. However, postponing means paying additional money.

The overwhelming majority of pensioners suffers from malnutrition, i.e. they do not get enough food, in terms of both calories and nutritional value. Pensioners without family can hardly survive. They often get food from neighbours. A small number of pensioners, approximately 5 - 10 per cent, live in homes for the elderly where they share a room with other pensioners and care is on an extremely low level. Formerly, old people had a lot of privileges, for example, reductions for all kinds of public services. Up to 1997, public transport was free for pensioners. All these privileges have been abolished, even applied for the veterans of the 'Great Patriotic War'.

Pensioners have less opportunities to earn money. Many pensioners spend long hours in the bazaar trying to sell some small things. Whereas in the early 1990s only some *baboesjkas* sold sunflower seeds, by the mid-1990s a whole army of them appeared. Often, in winter, old women spend long days in extreme cold on the streets to earn a little bit to survive. Some are dying on the streets. From the mid-1990s onwards, one can see a lot of pensioners looking for food in the garbage containers. Among the beggars in Zaporizhzhya, there are many pensioners.

Services for pensioners are very badly organised. In each residential district there is an office where pensions are allocated. When something is changed in the pension, for example when their partner dies, the pensioner must go to this office. However, these offices are understaffed and services are bad. Pensioners have to queue for many hours, often in winter standing in the cold. It is torture and sometimes leads to deaths. In many cases pensioners refrain from arranging a higher pension, out of fear of the administrative red tape and queuing.

Older people were the first to be fired when enterprises had to economise on personnel. This made them feel superfluous. Generally, aged people could morally not adjust to the new situation. The majority of the older generation believed in communism and now they are faced with the restoration of wild capitalism, private property, jungle individualism and the power of Ukrainian nationalism. Everything for which they stood is a lost cause and this contributes to their despair. During the wave of hyper-inflation, in 1993 - 1994, pensioners lost their savings. When, on top of that, in 1995 - 1996 the payment of pensions was often postponed in Zaporizhzhya, a wave of suicides among pensioners occurred.

The disabled

The situation for the disabled has become desperate in Zaporizhzhya. They were the first to be fired and special facilities to employ the disabled were abolished. For example, in a local bottle factory a department for making corks where disabled people worked closed. Also, a special department for blind and deaf persons in Avtozaz closed.

Disabled people who live in one of the twelve special houses face a horrible fate. These houses face a lack of money and there is not even enough food. One positive change is that recently all disabled people received a right to claim a pension. Nevertheless, their general situtation has worsened due to declining medical care and other services.

Generally, the disabled are systematically excluded from society.[7] The policy in Soviet times had always been to isolate the disabled in special houses located far from towns. The disabled, even those with a minor disability and who are able to work, face great problems in getting a job. A brilliant mathematician who finished the specialised mathematical school with a gold medal, could not study at the Technical University and could not get a job because he was lame. After emigration to Israel he immediately began a brilliant career.

In Zaporizhzhya there are no facilities for the disabled. One rarely sees them on the street. Their mobility is aided with only extremely primitive equipment. No wheelchairs can be seen in Zaporizhzhya.

Many people have become disabled at the workplace due to negligence and outmoded equipment. The metallurgical enterprises have become especially dangerous places to work. For many years hardly anything has been invested with a very negative impact upon safety. Because people are desperate, safety norms are often neglected. Usually, people who become disabled at the workplace cannot claim any benefits from the enterprise, because it is difficult to prove that the enterprise is to blame for the accident. Employees are usually quite powerless with regard to their employers, despite the existence of trade unions. For example, when a employee of Zaporozhstal died as a result of an explosion, only the funeral was paid for, apart from a small allowance for his child.

The number of fatal injuries in the workplace decreased in Zaporizhzhya province from 101 in 1990 to 74 in 1995. The decline is not surprising given the fact that industrial decline in that period has been approximately 60 - 70 per cent and more than half of the industrial labour force became *de facto* unemployed. Given the latter figures, the decline in fatal injuries has been low and the rate of fatal injuries related to actual working days has risen sharply.

The total number of fatal injuries was in Ukraine in 1990 2600. As Zaporizhzhya has 4 per cent of the Ukrainian population, the expected number of fatal injuries for Zaporizhzhya would be 104. It means that, in 1990, the rate of fatal injuries in Zaporizhzhya was close to the national average. However, the rate of fatal injuries has been many times higher compared to Western European countries. If we compare with the United Kingdom and Italy, countries of similar size the number of fatal injuries have been in 1994 respectively 211 and 956, whereas in Ukraine in 1994 there were 2300 fatal injuries.[8]

Orphans and abandoned children

The number of abandoned children and orphans increased dramatically with the economic crisis. These children used to go to boarding schools and sanatoriums. Now the best of these boarding schools and most of these sanatoriums are closed. For example, the big boarding school on the island Hortitsa is now closed and the building sold to a commercial enterprise.

Many mothers abandon their children. In the 1970s a law was issued that lifted the punishment for this. Since then mothers can leave their children without fear at special homes for babies. But still some women drop their babies in garbage containers.

Fewer couples can afford to adopt orphans, while there are more mothers, or couples, that do not want to keep their babies. The result is that the number of abandoned children has increased drastically. Most of the babies in the special homes have some kind of defect. The development of these children is retarded very much as no one takes care of their special needs. When visiting a kindergarten for orphans, or the special houses for children, the children are screaming 'Papa' or 'Mama' in the hope that someone will take them away.

Many children in orphanages actually have parents, but they are, for example, alcoholics who maltreated their children. Often these children became beggars and began to live on the streets, perhaps because their parents sold their house to obtain money in order to buy alcohol. This happened quite often and therefore a law was issued that prevented parents with children up to 18 years old from selling their apartment.

The children houses, as well as the boarding schools, are so poor that there is not even enough money for decent clothes. As more facilities for abandoned children and orphans close, more children appear as beggars and vagrants on Zaporizhzhya streets. Many of these children gather in public places like railway stations. Many children are ordered by their parents, often alcoholics, to beg and sing in order to earn money.

Sport

In Soviet times there was an extended infrastructure for sport including specialised sport schools that were free of charge and a large number of sport halls and swimming pools. Zaporizhzhya had a good name in a number of sports. The Zaporizhzhya women's handball team was famous all over the former Soviet Union.

With the economic crisis this infrastructure broke down. Almost all sport schools are closed and reknowned trainers are unemployed. All sport complexes are in very bad condition. Some of these complexes have been transformed into facilities for the new rich with saunas and luxury bars.

Public housing

Housing has always been one of the main problems of Zaporizhzhya. Nowadays, many families, i.e. approximately 20 per cent, still live in *kommunalkas*, that means they share the apartment with other families. From the early 1990s the building of houses, other than for the new rich, gradually came to a halt.[9] Apart from lack of money, this also was related to corruption. It regularly happened that money was collected to build flats, and then subsequently the construction would come to a halt because allocated funds and materials disappeared.

From the mid-1980s the housing stock had hardly been maintained. This means that the decay of the larger part of the housing stock is in an advanced stage. Also a great number of people who bought a house do not have enough money to maintain a house. This means that many houses have become unhabitable and that in the larger part of Zaporizhzhya houses are in danger of becoming unhabitable.

The majority of people can not pay for their rent and housing services. Owners of houses have to pay such high taxes that ownership becomes a fiction. If owners of private houses cannot pay for taxes and housing services, the municipality may forbid the sale of the house and may claim part of the house. The municipality still pays for the larger part of housing services. But the population cannot even pay for subsidised rents and housing services. Up to now, the municipality did not expel people from their houses. However, a silent war between local authorities and the population developed as the authorities resorted increasingly to sanctions, for example, cutting the electricity or warm water supply.

During the last few years, it more often happened that people bought private apartments and forced tenants to leave the apartment as a result of which the tenant became homeless. Homelessness has not become a widespread phenomenon, although some families live in the sewage system or subways of Zaporizhzhya. But massive homelessness hangs as a sword of

Damocles above Zaporizhzhya as more people are not able to pay their rent and house owners will resort to more drastic measures to get non-paying tenants out.

Communication and transport infrastructure

In Zaporizhzhya there is a very heavy reliance, by Western standards, on railway transport (17.5 million tonnes in 1994). One should know that generally, the Ukrainian economy is very much reliant upon rail transport. Italy, the UK, Germany and France combined transported only 60 per cent of freight by train compared to the Ukraine in 1993.[10] However, for many years practically nothing has been invested in railways. The result is that the speed of trains has to be reduced continuously due to bad condition of rails.

Road freight transport only accounted for 6.5 million tonnes and river transport 2.5 million tonnes. This is remarkable considering, for Ukrainian and Russian standards, the good highway connections and excellent water connections to the North and the South.

Zaporizhzhya has an airport that was intensively used in Soviet times. However, since the independence of Ukraine the amount of passengers dropped by more than ten times.[11] More passengers take the train.[12]

Public transport within Zaporizhzhya province is of very low quality. Due to lack of investment fewer trains are running although there is less of a drop in demand. The speed of passenger trains has been reduced. For example, going from Zaporizhzhya to Orechov, a town of about 20,000 inhabitants, 50 km from Zaporizhzhya, takes 2 hours 40 minutes (on average), while five years ago the same distance took 1 hour 40 minutes. Also within Zaporizhzhya town there is a deterioration of public transport, affecting economic life very much.

The municipality increasingly uses expensive bus services to replace normal bus and tram lines. For example, after a large number of people blocked the road in Baburka, a remote residential district, because public transport was unreliable and often people appeared too late for work, the municipality installed an expensive bus line for which people have to pay 60 kopecks or more instead of the previous 20 kopecks. Many people are dependent on such expensive transport and spend a large part of their salary for it. Taxis in Zaporizhzhya are expensive although fares have become cheaper since more private taxis appeared since early 1996. More competition has lead to lower tariffs. But still, few can afford taxis and they are difficult to find. Increasingly, reliable public transport becomes something only for the well-to-do people.[13]

Also, since 1995, public transport is controlled by conductors and police. In former times, people threw money in a box and took a ticket. In those times there was no control.

The main problem with communication is the bad telephone infrastructure. Telephone switchboards date from the period just after World War II. With the normal telephone network it is extremely difficult to communicate. For most small and medium-sized enterprises, leased lines and mobile telephone connections still are too expensive.[14] It is next to impossible to get new telephone service of any quality from the government telephone services. One has to wait more than five years after application before one gets a telephone connection. Only if one pays 500 dollars can one get immediately a connection.

Computer networking, in particular e-mail, may, in principle, solve many communication problems, but again, bad telephone lines slow any real progress.

Computer networking may also relieve the very poor level of information supply in Zaporizhzhya. However, only institutions can afford this. Again, on-line connection with the Internet is too expensive and difficult due to poor quality telephone lines. Nevertheless, by the mid-1990s, the number of Internet hosts began to increase rapidly in Zaporizhzhya, though the development of computer networking in Zaporizhzhya seem to have developed despite the inactivity of public authorities.[15]

In Zaporizhzhya, much more so compared to Western countries, a society of two speeds is developing, the extremely low speed (the train to Orechov) and the extremely high speed (those having access to Internet).

The disintegration of other municipal services

Formerly, municipal services cleaned and maintained public roads and parks and regularly collected rubbish. Nowadays, these services are malfunctioning or absent with the result that Zaporizhzhya has become a rather dirty town. One can smell the overflowing garbage containers everywhere. Roads are dustier than before.

Kindergarten, for children from 3 to 6 years, and crèches, for children from 1 to 3 years, that belonged to the big plants, have usually been sold and children have been sent to poorer municipal kindergartens. Most crèches have been closed. The nurses and teachers of the closed crèches and kindergartens are usually unemployed.

There used to exist a well-developed chain of milk-kitchen shops, where mothers could get cheap dairy products for their children. Also, baby food shops existed. These facilities gradually disappeared. Nowadays, expensive imported child food and milk powder have to be bought in the normal shops. Also, laundrettes, cleaning services and numerous other services have disappeared.

In Soviet times there was a peculiar kind of 'public service' that was quite essential to preserve the general level of public services. The Communist Party was the central organiser of society. Soviet society can be considered as a mono-organisational society, as the party did not allow independent organisations to exist. The party's function was also to make sure things got done in society. If citizens were faced with a hole in the roof of their apartment that needed urgent repair, they used to call the district party office that took care of rapid repair. If there were problems with the supply of goods of industrial enterprises, the local party organisation could help. The party functioned as oil in this highly bureaucratised society.

With the disintegration of the Communist Party, it was not only a repressive apparatus that fell away, but also a moving force behind society.

Conclusion

Generally, the extended public services network that developed in Soviet times, and that used to be very cheap or free of charge, has collapsed. This has especially affected the poor, that is, the majority of the population. The extended public service sector can be seen as the accumulated wealth of several generations that constitutes an infrastructure for the creation of wealth for future generations. This has been broken down in a historically very short period.

When calculating the extent of the economic crisis in Ukraine, economists and politicians mostly look at the development of the purchasing power of people's salaries, that has declined dramatically in Ukraine, to industrial decline or decline of Gross Domestic Product. They usually do not take into consideration the above described disintegration of the extended network of public services from which all Ukrainians used to profit.

Notes

1. Whereas the United States has spend more than 14 per cent of GDP on health care, Germany 10.4 per cent and France 9.8 per cent, the Soviet Union spent 6.6 per cent of GDP on health care in 1965, 4.1 per cent in 1970 and 3.3 per cent in 1980. It rose to 3.4 per cent in 1989. In Central European countries, expenses for health care were by the mid-1990s on average 5.9 per cent of GDP. (Millar, Wolchik, p. 179 and *The Economist*, 14 June 1997).
2. Free services were not really free, as the system of presents for doctors, to ensure good treatment, spread since the mid-1960s.
3. Only 18 per cent of Ukrainian women utilise mechanical means of contraception and only 3.5 per cent oral means (United Nations, 1996).
4. *Delovaya Ukraina*, 15 November 1995, p.1,2.
5. Zaporizke 1996b, p.19.
6. Museum visits increased, from 25 per 100 inhabitants in 1990 to 28 per 100 inhabitants in 1995.
7. When a couple has a disabled child, in most cases the man divorces.
8. *Yearbook of Labour Statistics* (ILO), 1996.
9. Whereas in 1992 in Zaporizhzhya province 682,000 square metres housing space has been built, in 1995 the newly-built housing space has declined to 90,000 square metres.
10. *Ekonomika Ukraina*, November 1995, p. 17.
11. Whereas there were in 1991 434,000 passengers in Zaporizhzhya airport, in 1995 this number had declined to 40,700.
12. The number of train passengers in Zaporizhzhya province increased from 19.6 million in 1991 to 25.3 million in 1995. The number of passengers in Zaporizhzhya trolley buses declined from 74.8 million passengers in 1991 to 20.5 million passengers in 1995. The number of tram passengers declined in the same period from 73.2 million passengers to 18.4 million passengers.
13. In Zaporizhzhya, trams and buses are completely unreliable. Going from one corner of the centre (Lenin Avenue) to the other corner of the centre (the same Lenin Avenue), a distance of about 8 kilometres, may take on average about one hour. However, it often happens that it takes 1.5 hours or even 2 hours. It means that it is very difficult to keep appointments if dependent on public transport.
14. A mobile telephone apparatus costs in Zaporizhzhya around 600 dollars. A telephone connection costs 500 dollars.
15. Shortly after the University of Zaporizhzhya got its homepage on Internet, an American businessman contacted the University with the proposal to co-operate in the development of software. When a German enterprise had to find a partner in Ukraine for a TEMPUS project, it selected four universities in Ukraine with a homepage. The University of Zaporizhzhya was the first to respond and got the project, an example of how the Internet may be profitable for Zaporizhzhya.

8 Social Change

In previous chapters major changes in Zaporizhzhya have been described such as the Ukrainisation of Zaporizhzhya, the transition to another economic system, the emergence of a new political system as well as the decline of industry and agriculture. In this chapter changes in society at large will be discussed, more in particular changing values and norms and changing relations between and within various social groups.

The Stalinist socio-psychological syndrome

Zaporizhzhya society can be described as a product of the history of social relations in Zaporizhzhya. This history is reflected in the individuals that constitute together Zaporizhzhya society. Although differences between individuals in Zaporizhzhya are as large as in any other place in the world, most inhabitants of Zaporizhzhya exhibit a coherent set of attitudes that has developed under tsarist and communist rule (see Appendix 1).

The communist and tsarist past has produced a system of values, norms and behavioural patterns that is quite persistent and that is able to reproduce itself. The properties of the syndrome can be summarised in the following way: the tsarist and communist past have created a cult of power that made the attribute of power, and therewith also the lack of it, of overriding importance in social life. Absolutist power was the rule. Self-organisation of society was almost absent, also in tsarist times. Later, the wish of the party-state to control all aspects of social life produced a control mania. A correlative is the aversion to delegating power and with employees, an aversion to assuming responsibility. Initiative was not rewarded but punished. Independent thinking was discouraged, also in the universities. The party-state promoted a simplistic world outlook, based on exclusion, i.e. all opinions other than that of the party are not true. The state, in principle, took care of almost everything in the individual's life - there was care from cradle to grave, eliciting a general passivity.

The disregard for truth in public life, absolutist power and lawlessness created distrust in public life. In recruitment mechanisms for influential posts, the Nomenklature system, loyalty was of primordial importance, less so competence. This furthered incompetence on all levels. Competent people were often marginalised. The primordial importance of obedience created people that comply with everything that is imposed upon them.

Though the properties attributed to the Stalinist socio-psychological syndrome became most pronounced in Stalin's time, many of these properties had already developed in tsarist times and are described in 19th-century Russian literature.[1] Six years after the independence of Ukraine and the dissolution of the Soviet empire it appears that this syndrome is very persistent and that Homo Sovieticus[2] is still very much alive. Nevertheless, with transition to the market economy the circumstances in which Zaporizhzhya citizens lived changed fundamentally. Skills, values and coping strategies developed in earlier decades have proved vastly inadequate.

First of all there is the free-fall from what was care from birth to death to complete existential uncertainty. Nothing is certain anymore. There has been a changeover from a planned life in which almost no personal initiative was required to a life in which the individual's own initiative is crucial for survival. The result is not an outburst of entrepreneurial activity, producing new goods and services, but a defensive reaction, retreating into familiar activities, such as the cultivation of ones own garden and selling of its products, or the extension of the system of services among friends that already existed before the collapse of communism. The visible effect is that of the phenomenal growth of the bazaar. When someone has not got money anymore, the first activity is to sell property on the bazaar.

This reaction is usually not adequate. The majority of people have been pushed into primitive forms of economy as their income is not enough for a decent life. The correlative of the above described changes is despair and passiveness. People cannot cope anymore with new circumstances and are afraid for the future. The result is, among others, that traditional forms of escapism, to escape from the sufferings of everyday life, become more pronounced. Alcoholism has spread even more and the use of hard drugs has become wide spread among the youth.

Another element that gradually became apparent in the transition process, but that developed under communism, is that of a moral disorientation and moral vacuum. It seems that in Soviet times the totalitarian power of the party-state prevented people from doing things that are generally considered to be amoral, such as stealing. As this totalitarian power vanished and was not replaced by another external disciplining power it appeared that many people lost the feeling for what is wrong and right. The rapid spread of what is considered amoral behaviour is probably not only related to the lawlessness in society that enabled criminal behaviour to spread but also to the lack of a moral disciplining force for concerned individuals. Social institutions that have traditionally helped to hold deviant behaviour in check have themselves weakened or been undermined. Apart from the collapse of the coercive force of the party-state, there is the authority of the family that decreased, also related to the rise of one-parent families. The collapse of formal controls has exacerbated the collapse of social controls.

The issue of theft is an interesting one. Stealing state property never has been seen by the wider public as amoral behaviour. Stealing from the state was not really deviant behaviour. The adage was 'if you do not steal from the state, you steal from your family'. Stealing state property became gradually more widespread in Soviet times. Of course, stealing from private citizens was considered amoral. Nevertheless, with 'liberalisation', private appropriation of state property became widespread, and this massive theft of state property was enabled by the leniency with regard to it.

Another issue is that of lying. Generally, under Soviet rule people became very tolerant towards lying as the state asked the people to lie in public. The tolerance towards not speaking the truth helped to create the present widespread distrust in public life that increases enormously transaction costs in the economy.

The impoverishment of the population and the rise of a predatory ruling class has enabled the emergence of a merciless society in which the common good has low value. There has been a change from an over-regulated society with strong social control, towards a society in which jungle individualism is predominant. Generally, interactions between citizens have become more rude. Related to impoverishment and moral vacuum, the search for money has become of overriding importance for a large part of the young generation. Everything should be paid for, even the smallest services.

In present social upheavals, it seems that the norms of the underworld have become those of the elite and therefore more prominent.

Generally, the individual's reaction on deteriorating living circumstances and the collapse of the environment that has produced the Stalinist socio-psychological syndrome is a defensive one. Market theorists from the West assumed that if the market was introduced in the East, market forces would function as a crowbar to force a modern market economy to develop. Apart from the fact that real markets hardly developed in

Zaporizhzhya, the assumption that, if the market mechanism really was in place people would react in Zaporizhzhya as they do in the West, is doubtful. The collapse of the party-state allowed a kleptocracy to develop, not a market economy.

There is a complex interrelationship between changing environment and the mentality of the people. The development of a kleptocracy is made possible partly because people, the victims, allowed it to develop. Oppressor and victim form a kind of symbiosis. In the West the opinion is still widespread that it is possible to introduce market economies and parliamentary democracies as are known in the West by decree - by the government's act to introduce a new regulatory mechanism. It is a voluntarist assumption.

It is maintained here that social and economic development of Zaporizhzhya society and economy is path-dependent. Alternative development paths may be within a set of constraints that exclude other development paths. The Stalinist socio-psychological syndrome, together with many other constraining factors, such as the lack of experience with market economy and parliamentary democracy and present social structures, prevent the development of a Western-style democracy or Western-style market economy in the short or medium term. Although eroding, the Stalinist socio-psychological syndrome is persistent and can not be eradicated in the lifespan of one generation.

The Stalinist socio-psychological syndrome furthers authoritarianism and semi-feudal ways of governing. It is an obstacle to the development of rule of law and economic development.

Stalinist rule, and more general, the whole history of tsarist and communist rule, is reflected in the mental set-up of people in Zaporizhzhya.[3] It has become part of the accumulated historical experience that is reflected in each individual that has grown up in Zaporizhzhya society. In other words, the Stalinist system has to a certain extent been internalised.

The spread of crime

During Perestroika, above all since 1989, criminality spread rapidly. Since independence this trend continued. The year 1996 showed an especially rapid rise in the crime rate.[4] The murder rate increased from 9 per 100,000 in 1990 to 21 per 100,000 in 1995. This rate is extremely high and more than 23 times as high as in Britain and more than 7 times as high as in Italy in 1992.[5]

Generally, breaking the law has been gradually punished less. Whereas in 1990 out of 1003 discovered road accidents 1099 persons were convicted, in 1995 out of 507 discovered road accidents 99 were convicted. These figures make it plausible to state that, due to bribery, less road accidents have been reported, and, again related to corruption of judges, less people are convicted.

The general lawlessness in society enabled crime to spread rapidly. Criminals bribe the police in order not to be persecuted. In 1994, in more than half of all murder cases, the defendants were freed. Also, criminals are usually better armed than the police. As crooks have little chance to be captured by the police or judicial authorities and the rewards are great, the sphere of crime has attracted many. Crime in Zaporizhzhya is not dominated by a big Mafia, but rather well-organised by small gangs, none of which is dominant, terrorising society.

Of course, there is also large-scale crime in the form of the illegal appropriation of state property. The point is that in ruling circles this is not considered to be a crime, just as the criminal state power in Stalin's time was not seen as criminal by the majority of people.

What is new is that the state no longer has the monopoly over arbitrary violence. The new violence of criminal bands is more unpredictable and makes everyday life less safe. The spread of crime has to a great extent influenced the daily life of Zaporizhzhya citizens. It has become dangerous, especially when it is dark, to be on the streets. Bands attack people even at daytime, without being afraid of being caught by police. The police is itself part of the problem as corrupt officers try to extract as much money from citizens as possible.

Social inequalities

It is the passivity of the general population that has allowed a predatory ruling class, described in Chapter 4, to appropriate an ever-larger share of the ever-smaller cake of Zaporizhzhya wealth.

As anywhere else in Ukraine, income disparities have grown enormously during transition and nowadays Ukraine is on a par with the European countries experiencing the largest income disparities.

In Zaporizhzhya this process has become visible in the emergence of a class of new rich that are very rich, comprising about 5 - 10 per cent of the population. In it are merchants that have become rich, bankers, the upper management of large state enterprises and politicians. This class has accumulated so much wealth that prices are, for them, not important any more. They buy products in the new fashionable shops on Lenin Avenue or go to the disco where drinks are more expensive than in London or Paris discos. They have built villas in new residential areas that bear witness to their lack of taste.

Although the new rich may constitute approximately 10 per cent of the population in Zaporizhzhya town, i.e. about 100,000 persons, the wealth of this group hardly benefits cultural life.

On the other hand there is the overwhelming majority of the population that has become rapidly impoverished.[6] More than half of the population lives under the poverty line. That means that almost all their income has to be spend on food. The poor do not have the money to buy medicines or to pay for medical services.

For Zaporizhzhya, no data about poverty are available. In Kharkiv, the major town in Eastern Ukraine, an opinion poll conducted in September 1996 gives an indication of the situation in Zaporizhzhya; as we may assume that poverty in the two towns will not differ very much. Some 1,502 persons were interviewed. With respects to living standards five groups were distinguished. Forty-seven per cent of the respondents classified themselves in group A ('We do not have enough money even for staple foods'), 37 per cent in group B ('We spend all our wages on foodstuffs and essential inexpensive things'), 12 per cent in group C ('There is enough money in general, however, we can not afford any durable goods') and only 4 per cent in group D ('We are quite well-off'). It means that in Kharkiv, the overwhelming majority (84 per cent) is impoverished. The respondents were, among other questions, asked 'In your opinion what is your place in society now, which step on the social staircase do you occupy?' While in 1986, 85 per cent of respondents reckoned themselves to middle class, this declined in 1996 to 39 per cent. While 6 per cent of respondents reckoned themselves in 1986 to lower classes, this percentage was in 1996 49 per cent. It means that in terms of self-ascribed social status, the social stratification of the population of Kharkiv deteriorated enormously. The authors of the reports noticed that values that used to determine the respondents' social status, such as level of education and moral and human qualities, dropped considerably in their view, whereas such factors as level of income, personal connections and business qualities become more and more important.[7]

More than half of the population is *de facto* unemployed, that means that they have no regular income at all. They survive by selling products of their gardens or creating a network of services and counter-services among friends and families. Those having a garden are increasingly faced with theft of their crops. Also, for many it has become too expensive to travel regularly to their gardens.

For those who have a regular job, the second jobs are usually more important. An inquiry, at the end of 1994, in Ukraine found that of employed people, 54 per cent of total income is secondary income.[8]

Falling living standards have pushed many women into prostitution. Although prostitution occurs in all societies, in Soviet times prostitution was quite limited and not very much visible. Nowadays a large number of very young girls, i.e. from 12 years onwards, engage in prostitution. Tariffs become lower as competition among prostitutes grows. By 1997, girls were selling themselves for just more than a dollar.

Do men suffer more than women?

In Soviet times, public authorities stated that the women's question had been resolved. Practically all adult women worked. However, the majority of them had a double task in that they also did most of the housework. Thus, the traditional role division between the genders came under increasing stress with the emancipation of women.

Although there were not many women to be found at the commanding heights in economy and society, their chances in public life increased. Women became more self-confident. Women also had in most cases to show more initiative to secure the survival of the family. They provided a positive role model in most families. The social role model of the father was often reduced to the man lying on the sofa and reading the newspaper, not taking care of the children. Therefore, even when the father was physically present, there was often the absent father syndrome. Women are the major pillar of family life, that important bastion against the suffocating surrounding world. Even with their work overload Zaporizhzhya women try, in most cases, to preserve their feminine qualities. Despite their present poverty, many women reserve a considerable amount of their disposable income for cosmetics and fashionable clothes.

Box 8.1 A day in the life of a woman from Zaporizhzhya

Tatyana K. is thirty-seven years old. Married with two children. She has always lived in Zaporizhzhya. Tatyana graduated from the Zaporizhzhya Pedagogical Institute (nowadays the University) and works as a teacher in English.

Her fate and daily worries are very typical. Her long working life was not sufficient to get her own apartment or even decent furniture. She lives with her family in her mother's apartment. Her mother is a pensioner. Tatyana's husband worked as a truck driver for one of the big plants in Zaporizhzhya. Now this enterprise stands idle. Other employment is not available. As before, Tatyana's often drinks. The present difficult circumstances have made him a degraded alcoholic.

Tatyana, as most Ukrainian women, feels herself responsible for the fate of her children. She is accustomed to solve all family problems on her own. If her husband cannot be a normal father, mother will take over his function. Her eldest daughter studies at the Kyiv school for artistic talented children. This is financially a heavy burden, because the whole family lives on Tatyana's income. Apart from her son and daughter, Tatyana also takes care of a niece who studies at one of Zaporizhzhya's schools.

Tatyana's working day starts at half past seven and ends late in the evening, sometimes midnight. She is a good and creative teacher, but her day is overburdened. The lessons begin each day at ten past eight. At that time Tatyana is ready to receive her pupils with a smile and a laugh. Every day she has six to eight lessons, but after these her work is not yet finished. Tatyana is the class leader of the ninth form. She has to check in the course of the day whether all the teachers of her class will be present, she must write down in the class book the absent pupils, she makes at the end of each trimester a progress report for all pupils of her class, she has to speak every day with the teachers of her class in order to remain informed about all the events in her class and to know about the successes and problems of each of the thirty-five pupils. And this is not all. Every two or three weeks her class has school service, that means that everybody in class should maintain order in the school, under her supervision, from half past seven in the morning till eight o'clock in the evening.

With such a working day she can not even take a rest in the breaks between the lessons. Moreover, Tatyana must make an assessment of each pupil and fill in the school forms every week. Not less than once in every three weeks she must prepare a performance or another out-of-class event, as well as organising a parent's meeting each trimester.

All this work, except the lessons, are almost without payment, but refusal is impossible for most of the teachers, because a 'rebel' will immediately be replaced by another teacher who will be happy to take over the job.

To find a job in a good school and not far from home is very difficult. Therefore Tatyana appreciates her job. She frees times for meetings and phone calls with the parents of her pupils, for the correction of pupil's work, for the reading of new books about didactics, psychology and novels, to prepare an interesting contribution for the school board or the professional teachers' meeting. All household work, such as shopping, cooking and cleaning, is also her job.

As a teacher Tatyana has a modest salary. That is, of course, not even enough to buy normal food for the family. Therefore Tatyana has private lessons. Here she is a happy exception among her colleagues, as in present circumstances only teachers in her speciality can find pupils among the potential emigrants and the children of the new rich, who need English, in order to study abroad. Private lessons save her from deep misery, but not from poverty. And it costs her: Tatyana has serious health problems. A few years ago she had an operation, but she is full of inexhaustable energy. She fights for the health of her husband, strives after a good education for her children, helps her sister, who lives in even greater poverty. She does not feel herself unhappy. One can wonder about her exceptional energy and optimism. And here arises the question: how long will her strength last?

In summertime she usually works in a health camp. It is the only opportunity for a cure for her children, whom she can take with her as tutor of the camp. So, while working, she spends her holidays. Tatyana has never had a real opportunity to rest.

Tatyana is not an exception. Many women in Zaporizhzhya live in even worse conditions. What awaits them? Will their lives ever be organised in a normal and decent way? It is difficult to speak about it, but soon Tatyana's daughter may await the same fate.

Also, many women seem to be better educated than men, not because women have on average a better formal education, but because they often succeed in maintaining and improving their educational level after finishing school whereas men often do not. The problem with men is that they often become alcohol- dependent and as a result their qualifications suffered.

In Soviet times a very strict division developed between private life and public life. In private life women dominated and they constituted the backbone of private society. It was in private society that traditional values could be, to a certain extent, preserved and reproduced. It was the family, the micro-cosm of society, that was the core of the social reproduction process of society. At the same time it was separated from society at large.

Public life was the domain of men. It was also the domain of the lie, the domain in which one had to be very suspicious. In public life most people could not realise themselves. Public life was very authoritarian and not geared towards the full development of individuals. Although the former Soviet Union counted many well-educated women and men, few could fully use their intellectual potential at the workplace, and more generally, in public life. It meant that life in the public sphere, the primary domain of men, was quite frustrating. It is also in the public sphere that, as in most other countries, male values can be most easily realised. Men, in Soviet society, in most cases never have been masters of their own life.

A big problem developed in the sphere of masculinity and, as a consequence, in the relationship between the genders. Although the major burden of reproduction of society (in terms of workload) was for women, men seemed to suffer more. It is conspicuous to see that during the recent social and economic upheavals, the mortality rate of men rose drastically, but that of women hardly at all (see Chapter 10, section 2). Especially men in the age category 40 - 60 died - they had the greatest problems in adjusting to the new circumstances. Previously, their main role in family life was to bring in money. As many men become unemployed, their self-esteem has declined even more. They feel bereft of their dignity and become full outsiders, in both the family and in working life. They often become parasites and are treated as such by their wives. This usually results in increasing escapism and passivity.

Nowadays, the mortality rate of men is on the level of many less-developed countries.

Already under Soviet rule the divorce rate was climbing. Usually women took the initiative and it was mostly the women who took care of the children after divorce. The number of divorces has increased recently and the number of one-parent families has become very high.[9] Therefore, a large number of children grow up in families where the father is absent.

With increasing poverty, in many families both parents must spend more energy earning money. Children are often left without supervision. Combined with the disintegration of external social control, a great number of youths are exposed to the temptations of hooliganism, drugs and alcoholism.

Young people

Older generations grew up in a situation in which almost everything was arranged for them, and the state took care of them from birth to death. The new generation is the first one to be confronted with existential uncertainty on all levels. It means that they more easily adjust to the new situation and show more initiative than older people. It is above all young people that have success in the new commercial structures - they best understand the new economic and social laws. However, there is also a negative side in the sense that they also more easily accept the norms of the underworld. Nowadays, a considerable number of young people are obsessed by the search for money

Youth sub-cultures, similar to the one that spread in the Western world starting in the sixties, have spread gradually in Ukraine since the early 1970s. Generally, the extended network of educational and recreational facilities for young people that existed in Soviet times has disappeared.

Increasingly, since the 1960s, official ideology has had less impact upon young people and by the late 1980s they had become disillusioned with politics and widely dismissed socialism as an ideal. Gradually, more young people became ashamed about the past of their country and afraid of the future.

There is one great difference from young people in the Western world. Young people in Zaporizhzhya usually continue to live with their parents and are dependent, if they study, on their parent for support. This confines the limits of independent behaviour. Also the lack of money limits possibilities of participating in a youth culture.

Juvenile delinquency has spread since the late Brezhnev period, related to the falling away of traditional mechanisms of social control and spreading poverty. Deprived of social-level protection mechanisms, children and adolescents in particular are falling prey to drug abuse, alcohol and tobacco addiction, violence, child prostitution, sexually-transmitted diseases including AIDS, and crime.

Ethnic minorities

The position of the ethnic minorities in Zaporizhzhya changed greatly during recent social upheavals. Generally, they began to organise themselves better and ethnic identities became more pronounced.

Although to a lesser extent than in Western Ukraine, in Kyiv and in Kharkiv, Jews always have played an important role in the life of Zaporizhzhya, especially in trade, science and culture. About one-third of the population of Alexandrovsk consisted of Jews. They attached much importance to education. Therefore the level of education among Jews is much higher than within other ethnic groups.[10]

Starting in the early 1930s Jews went through a process of rapid assimilation related to the fact that it was not advantageous to be a Jew. For example, up to the late 1980s there were quota for Jews in higher education. In the early 1970s not more than 4 per cent of students in higher education could be Jews. Many Jews in Zaporizhzhya changed their names and passports in order to give themselves and their children better chances in social life.

As a result of opportunities to emigrate since the end of the 1970s, related to discrimination and economic crisis and because they were better informed about life abroad, many Jews emigrated to the United States, Israel, and, since 1991, also to Germany. This has meant a significant drain on intellectual resources of Zaporizhzhya. Nowadays, only about 2.5 per cent of the population of Zaporizhzhya town is Jewish.

Also, it became suddenly more advantageous to be a Jew and many people tried to prove that they were Jewish. Also, a Jewish community began to develop. Up to the late 1980s no genuine Jewish community existed in Zaporizhzhya as almost all Jews were assimilated, although often still recognisable. Since 1991 Jews began to organise themselves. A synagogue was opened and a Jewish school. Israel very actively stimulated Jewish life in Zaporizhzhya: Rabbis from Israel visited Zaporizhzhya and Jewish children from Zaporizhzhya were given the opportunity to study free in Israel. Those who wanted to emigrate to Israel were offered free tickets to Israel.

Many Jewish families in Zaporizhzhya now live separately: their children study in Israel, free of charge, while their parents continue to work in Zaporizhzhya because their prospects to find work in Zaporizhzhya are not so good.

The gypsy population of Zaporizhzhya amounts to several thousand persons. They live concentrated in one district of Zaporizhzhya are mainly active in trade. They are often prosecuted for petty theft and drugs trade. The gypsy minority is far less educated than the Ukrainian average and usually gypsies do not send their children to school. They are only to a minor extent integrated in Zaporizhzhya society.

Tartar settlements are to be found in Zaporizhzhya province and they have built a new mosque in the centre of Zaporizhzhya. There are also Germans in Zaporizhzhya, who came here during the colonisation of South-eastern Ukraine, although many among them emigrated. Germans have their own religious schools.

There are some Bulgarian villages in Zaporizhzhya province, where people still speak Bulgarian. However, gradually, Bulgarians lost their own schools. There are also Turkish communities and a small community of Assyrians, who locate their roots in the ancient Assyrian empire. They specialise in the jewel trade.

Conclusion

The collapse of the party-state, the main integration structure of society, has caused an integrational vacuum that is not filled by the structures of slowly developing civil society. This has caused anomie. Also, the lack of interest representation at the political level contributes to a jungle individualism that is in sharp contrast to the extreme social control during Soviet times. Reflexes of most individuals, especially the older ones, reflect tsarist and Soviet times when personal initiative was punished and compliance and passivity rewarded. Also, distrust in the public sphere was justified and disregard of the truth, if the state asked so, accepted. These reflexes are not adequate anymore and old behavioural routines constitute a tremendous barrier for the changeover to the modernisation of economy and society.

The crumbling of external social control furthered a moral vacuum and the spread of deviant behaviour. The crime explosion in Zaporizhzhya may be seen in this context.

The relation between men and women came under strain with the present social and economic crisis as the ability of men to bring in money for the family, their main function in the family, became endangered.

The spread of poverty affected the overwhelming majority of the population of Zaporizhzhya. By mid-1997, for a majority of people, even the securing of an adequate food supply is endangered. The spread of poverty is furthering crime and prostitution as well as drugs and alcohol abuse.

Notes

1. Gontsharov (*Oblomov*) can be mentioned, later Dostojevsky (*Demons*), Tsjechov (*The Cherry Orchard*) and Gogol (*Dead Souls*). In Soviet times Bulgakov (*The Master and Margerita*). The philosophers Berdjaev and Rosenov wrote extensively about the lack of initiative of the Russian intelligentsia.
2. With great reluctance we use the concept Homo Sovieticus, as this phenomenon existed already before 1917, although less pronounced.
3. Although during the Perestroika years quite a number of books appeared that revealed the crimes committed under Stalin, public debate about the causes of Stalinist rule remained quite limited.
4. Millar, pp. 131, 135. Whereas in 1990 7283 cases of petty theft were reported in Zaporizhzhya province, in 1994 the number of cases had increased to 11,737. The number of burglaries increased in that period from 977 to 1,796 cases. Fraud cases increased 2.5 fold. Cases of corruption increased from 15 in 1992 to 86 in 1994.
5. *Demographic Yearbook* 1994, p. 504. In 1993, the murder rate was in Ukraine 11.3 per 100,000.
6. The purchasing power of the general population declined drastically. Whereas in 1990 485,000 radios were sold in the shops, in 1994 the figure was only 75,000. 67,000 television sets were sold in 1990, in 1994 only 8,000. In 1990 1000 pianos have been sold, in 1994 none.
7. TACIS. EDUK 9402.
8. Johnson et al, 1996, p. 113. At the end of 1994 employed people earned on average $15.90 a month in their primary formal employment and $29.30 per month through secondary activities. The cost of a minimal survival basket of food per adult was about $30 per person.
9. The number of divorces increased in Zaporizhzhya from 9,598 in 1990 to 10,021 in 1995 whereas the number of marriages decreased from 20,381 in 1990 to 16,294 in 1994 (12,168 in 1996 on the basis of figures for the first half of the year).
10. Within Ukraine, on average 85 per 1000 persons of 15 years and older had higher education, the corresponding figure for Jews was 358 and for Russians 158 in Ukraine (*Human Development Report*).

9 An Ecological Crisis Zone

In the former Soviet Union, political leaders did not worry about environmental pollution. Increase of industrial output, in quantitative terms, was the main aim. Lack of environmental protection made the Soviet Union one of the most polluted countries in the world. Within the former Soviet Union, South-eastern Ukraine was one of the most polluted regions and Zaporizhzhya town was one of the most polluted towns.

Atmospheric pollution

Among 104 Soviet towns Zaporizhzhya was the 22nd most polluted town in 1988.[1] In 1995 Zaporizhzhya province expelled 268,785 tonnes of pollutants into the atmosphere.[2] This is the official figure. Actual figures are probably much higher. In Zaporizhzhya there is especially high atmospheric pollution including benzopyrene, carbon monoxide, sulfur dioxide, nitrogen dioxide, formaldehyde, dust and phenol.[3] Amongst the Ukrainian provinces, only Dnepropretovsk, Donetsk and Ivanofrankovsk have higher levels of atmospheric pollution.[4] Eighty-four per cent of emissions were from industrial enterprises and 16 per cent from cars in 1994. Of the industrial emissions, 83 per cent are on the account of heavy metallurgy.[5]

Zaporizhzhya has a high concentration of highly polluting industries, especially ferrous metallurgy and the very polluting Zaporozhkoks and Aluminium Enterprise.[6]

Also in the machine-building industry there are a lot of heavy polluters. The Dniprovsky Electrode Factory in Zaporizhzhya is responsible for only 3.5 per cent of pollutants being spewed out over the city. However, 80 per cent of them are carcinogenic and are ranked as highly dangerous.[7]

The polluting factories do not have adequate equipment to reduce environmental pollution. Untreated waste often enters the atmosphere. If there are filters, they are far from sufficient. There are sanctions on breaking the environmental rules. However, they do not function as enterprises simply do not pay the penalties or the penalties are so low that they do not function as sanctions.[8] A large number of environmental experts, that were in Soviet times employed in their speciality, can no longer find work in their field, due to a lack of funding.[9]

It is partly due to this absence of environmental protection that Zaporizhzhya producers of raw materials can still compete on world markets.

Among the factors contributing to high pollution levels is the fact that Ukrainian industry uses per capita more than 40 per cent more energy than in Western Europe. In Zaporizhzhya, industry often uses equipment dating from the 1930s.

Another problem in Zaporizhzhya is that industrial districts are close to the living quarters of the population. It is said that Stalin personally intervened in the physical planning of Zaporizhzhya, ordering that the industrial districts should be within walking distance of the living quarters of the workers. Therefore, the air in Zaporizhzhya is often unbearable.

Emissions of atmospheric pollutants have decreased in Zaporizhzhya due to sharply declining industrial production. But the decline in pollution is not equal to the decline in industrial activities. As a report of the Ministry of Environment observed, industrial emissions in Donetsk-Pridniprovsky region, including Zaporizhzhya province, remain relatively high: 'The share of these emissions reach 80 per cent of Ukrainian total amount.' The report noted that industrial emissions are especially high in Zaporizhzhya, Energodar and Mariupol.

Waste management

Generally, there is hardly any treatment of waste in Zaporizhzhya and there are particularly high levels of untreated chromium, cadmium and vanadium waste.

In Ukraine household waste is only 3 per cent of general waste, whereas this percentage is for Japan 19 per cent and for Germany 26 per cent. This is an indication for extremely inefficient use of resources in Ukraine.[10]

Also worrying is the deposit of untreated waste water into the River Dnepr. Of the 350,000 cubic metres of water coming daily into the Zaporizhzhya purification installations, 150,000 m3 is returned to the Dnepr untreated.[11] In 1995, a new purification station was under construction, but the money needed to complete this station is not available.[12]

Water pollution

The River Dnepr, streaming through Zaporizhzhya, is very polluted. Enterprises dispose of their waste by throwing all pollutants untreated in the Dnepr. Although industrial production declined sharply, due to worsening functioning of purification stations the amount of untreated waste thrown in the Dnepr increased from 816,000 tonnes in 1988 to 1,062,000 tonnes in 1994 (later figures are not available).[13]

According to a report in 1993, from 1991 to 1993 the quantity of zinc, copper, iron, magnesium, manganese, cadmium, nickel and lead increased by 50 per cent in the Dnepr near Zaporizhzhya.[14] It is in Zaporizhzhya that the Dnepr has the highest concentration of heavy metals.[15] The increase of chlorine, used in increasing quantities for the purification of water, has led to an increase of carcinogenic material, like trihalogen methane, in the Dnepr. Forty-three per cent of Dnepr water tests near Zaporizhzhya showed above normal salmonella and cholera contamination.[16] Dnepr water contains many mutagenic materials. According to a report published in 1991, Dnepr water just above Zaporizhzhya contained 2.4 times the norm for nitrates, 4 to 5 times the norm for faecal material, 4.4 to 4.8 times the norm for oil products and 6 to 7 times the norm for pesticides. Just below Zaporizhzhya these acceptable rates have been exceeded even more.[17]

Fishing nets used in the Dnepr near Zaporizhzhya, showed that the threads of the nets became ten times thicker as a result of oil products. The self-purification capacity of the Dnepr has been reduced dramatically. Dnepr water contains less than half the needed oxygen needed for a normal level of self-purification and is in danger of becoming a dead river.[18]

There is also in Zaporizhzhya bacteriological contamination of inland water bodies being in direct human use.[19] Therefore the municipality of Zaporizhzhya in 1994 forbade the population to bath in the Dnepr.

Remarkably the bacteriologial contamination of Dnepr has increased dramatically since 1980. Whereas Dnepr water contained in that year on average 17,000 micro organisms per liter, in 1988 the number had increased to 34,000.[20]

A telling example of pollution in Zaporizhzhya province is the decline of fish catch in Dnepr. In 1990 27 thousand tonnes were caught, while in 1994 only 11.9 thousand tonnes were landed.[21] This decline is due to environmental pollution, lessening control on the fish catch and overfishing. Also, the fish are often diseased and generally not fit for human consumption. The fish often have a high mercury content. Specialists advise the population to consume Dnepr fish not more than once a month.[22]

Zaporizhzhya is the only province in Ukraine that solely relies on Dnepr water for the provision of drinking water. Drinking water is not adequately purified. Therefore, drinking water is not potable; even boiling the water is not sufficient as it is contaminated with heavy metals and radionuclides. Chlorination of drinking water caused problems as the chlorine reacted with remnants of pesticides, creating dangerous material. Nowadays purification is furthered by the use of aluminium sulfide and silicic acid, the combination of which may cause mental retardation and even debility in children.[23] Regularly, local authorities warn of contamination with the Hepatitus A virus.

A survey of drinking water in Zaporizhzhya province in 1994 showed that 86 per cent of all tests showed drinking water of insufficient quality.[24]

Soil quality

In the 1950s and 1960s about 100,000 ha of less productive soils have been brought into cultivation in Zaporizhzhya province without bothering about protection of soils.[25] As a result, especially through wind erosion, the ecological balance has been distorted. In the last decade this process has been accelerated: 25 per cent more soil has disappeared through erosion than in the preceding ten years. The humus content of the upper layer of the soils has diminished drastically and the structure has deteriorated.

In the Donetsk Dnipro region, including Zaporizhzhya, 71 per cent of arable land is in a degraded condition. Soil is contaminated by remnants of fertilizers and pecticides. The area of acid and salinated soils has increased over the past 25 years by approximately 25 per cent.

In the orchards of Zaporizhzhya, heavy contamination with zinc and copper has been observed (respectively 2.2 and 2.3 times the maximum level).

Nuclear power

A major environmental concern in Zaporizhzhya, especially after the nuclear disaster in Chernobyl in 1986, is the nuclear power station in Energodar, 50 kilometres from Zaporizhzhya. The power station is of the VVER-1000 type and is the largest nuclear power station in Europe. It came on line in 1985. In 1995, after the moratorium on the expansion of nuclear power stations in Ukraine has been lifted, a sixth power block has been put into operation.[26] Nowadays Zaporizhzhya provides 33 per cent of all the nuclear power produced in Ukraine. It is a strategic station as it provides energy for the industrial Eastern Ukraine. Nuclear energy accounts for half of the total electrical energy produced in Ukraine.

As Ukraine is very much dependent on imports of gas and oil and as Ukraine's coal industry is loss-making, Ukrainian government attaches great importance to nuclear power, especially in these times of economic crisis.

Western countries are putting a lot of pressure upon the Ukrainian government to close Chernobyl and to introduce adequate safety measures in nuclear power stations. Huge amounts of money have been allocated by Western governments and institutions to this end. The nuclear power station of Zaporizhzhya has also been included in assistance schemes.[27]

The nuclear power station in Zaporizhzhya has the same flaws as other Soviet-type reactors. The plant has been placed in an area that has a high potential for flooding. The designers of the Zaporizhzhya plant did not have access to secret information concerning flooding scenarios until 1992. Despite international safety recommendations which suggest a maximum of four units at one site, Zaporizhzhya has a concentration of six nuclear units, thus making it the largest in Europe. Ukrainian requirements on population density within the 25-km zone are ignored. Zaporizhzhya, like all Ukrainian plants, has low-quality equipment that does not meet the current Ukrainian 'General Regulations on National Power Plants Safety', which, incidentally, are lower than most international requirements and recommendations in many respects.

Despite Western assistance, the general situation with respect to safety in the nuclear power station in Zaporizhzhya has not improved.[28] The nuclear power station does not have enough money for maintenance and repair of the station as only 50 per cent of delivered energy has been paid for.[29] Therefore the staff are not paid in time. Although these experts are on high salaries (seven times the Ukrainian average wage), many of them who received their training in Russia, went back to Russia as they are much better paid there. For example, in 1993 the plant lost 427 highly qualified workers, according to plant manager V. Bronnikov. In Ukraine as a whole, by mid-1994, Ukrainian plants had lost more than 8000 highly qualified specialists to Russia.[30] So, there is a huge problem of lack of competent personnel.

Box 9.1 A list of accidents in Zaporizhzhya nuclear power station

Reuters, 10 July 1996

A defective temperature gauge shut down a pump in a reactor undergoing maintenance at Ukraine's Zaporizhzhya nuclear power station.....but there is no radiation release, officials said on Wednesday.... It is said that the shutdown was caused by a defect in a temperature gauge in Zaporizhzhya's reactor number 1.

Reuters, 6 April 1996

A steam leak shut down a reactor at a station vital to Ukraine's delicate power grid, but there was no radiation escape and no environmental danger, officials said on Saturday.

Reuters, 4 March 1996

Snow whipped by winds gusting to 110 kph brought down two high-tension pylons near the Zaporizhzhya nuclear power station, Europe's largest, cutting capacity by 40 per cent in three of its six reactors.

Kievski Vedomosti, 12 February 1996.

A critical situation in Zaporizhzhya nuclear power station developed as Russia broke electrical energy ties with Ukraine and the nuclear power plant had to operate at a far too low level.

Reuters, 25 January 1996

The station in Zaporizhzhya has suffered technical problems, with the newest reactor shut down for 10 days less than a month after coming on stream..

Reuters, 5 January 1996

In one incident last month, a steam leak from a pump shut down one of six reactors at the Zaporizhzhya power plant, Europe's largest, but the steam did not escape from the reactor's containment vessel.

Reuters, 7 December 1995

A technical incident shut down a reactor at Ukraine's Zaporizhzhya nuclear power station for the second time this week..... The director of the affected reactor, the fifth of six 1,000 megawatt units at Europe's largest station, blamed the incident on a drop in water levels during a routine operation to cut capacity. This week's first stoppage severely hit electricity production and prompted Russia to decouple Ukraine from a joint power grid. The latest incident left only three reactors in operation - two were out of action following incidents and a third was undergoing scheduled maintenance. The incident was the third in a month at Zaporozhzhya, whose directors are coming under pressure to quit in view of their poor operating record.

Reuters, 16 November 1995

The sixth reactor at the Zaporizhzhya nuclear plant was shut down for 10 days after a small radio-active leak less than one month after being brought on steam.

Financial Times, 2 November 1995

A fire broke out in the Zaporizhzhya nuclear power station. The fire was contained to the station offices without endangering the station's five working reactors.

Reuters, 6 October 1995

A sixth reactor began working at the Zaporizhzhya nuclear power station... the newest reactor made the Zaporizhzhya station the largest in Europe and the third largest in the world.

Reuters, 4 December 1994

A steam leak from a pump shut down a reactor on Monday at the Zaporizhzhya nuclear power station ... the most trouble-prone of five [plants] in Ukraine. Ukraine's nuclear authority, said Zaporizhzhya had the largest number of incidents and 'anomalies' in the first six months of 1995 of five stations in the former Soviet republic.

Reuters, 16 November 1994

At the Zaporizhzhya station ... staff lost control of regulatory and security systems in one incident and a staff error prompted an unnecessary shutdown of a reactor in another.

UI News Briefing, 28 April 1994

Ukraine: An escape of radioactive steam which occurred during an overhaul at the Zaporizhzhya nuclear power station could rate as grade 3 on the INES scale. No date was given for the leak, which occurred when a valve regulating steam pressure failed to operate properly during a safety system test.

Reuters, Kiev, 8 March 1994

The fire at the Zaporizhzhya nuclear power station...raged about 600 metres from the main reactors for about an hour but was extinguished...

The plant has an impressive list of malfunctions. Between January 1990 and March 1994, 709 events were recorded (see Box 9.1).[31] In 1995 the plant had more malfunctions - 35 - than any other Ukrainian nuclear plant.[32] In that year only 54 per cent of the capacity of the power station has been used, due to malfunctions.

Around the nuclear power station international radiation safety levels are exceeded by a factor of 7.[33] In February 1996 the director of the plant was dismissed due to mismanagement.

A European Union-funded early warning system to detect increased radioactive levels in Ukraine was due to be in operation by mid-1996.

In Zaporizhzhya one has also felt the implications of the nuclear disaster at Chernobyl. Radioactivity levels of a lot of food products in Zaporizhzhya province increased suddenly to high levels. Whereas the contents of strontium-90 in milk was on average 1 times10(-12) ki per kilogram, it increased to 2.2 times in 1986, after the disaster. However, the level of Cesium-137 increased 1645 times. After 1986, radioactivity levels in most food products gradually diminished to pre-Chernobyl levels. However, fish from the Dnepr remained highly contaminated. Whereas the level of strontium-90 in Dnepr fish in Zaporizhzhya was 12.2 times 10(-12) ki per kilogram, it decreased to 5.5 just after the Chernobyl disaster, increased again to 88 in 1987 and subsequently gradually increased to a level of 126.5 in 1991 (later figures are not available). Whereas the level of Cesium-137 in 1985 in Dnepr fish has been 9.4 times 10(-12) ki per kilogram, it increased to 433 in 1986 (after the disaster) and thereafter gradually diminished, to a high level of 156 in 1991.[34]

Reactions of the public authorities and the general public

As will be shown in Chapter 10, a lot of diseases in Zaporizhzhya are caused by environmental pollution. The question arises what have public authorities done to improve the ecological situation in Zaporizhzhya.

In June 1994, a local district council near the nuclear power plant, put the question of the construction of the plants' unit 6 to voters. In two districts voters rejected the proposal. In the late 1980s the local authorities in Zaporizhzhya forbade the construction of new, and the extension of existing, industrial enterprises in Zaporizhzhya in order to prevent further pollution. However, this measure has never been followed up.[35] Early in 1994 a Department for Medical-Ecological Defence of the Population was opened in the municipality of Zaporizhzhya.[36] However, this department could not do much to improve the situation.

The public authorities have not taken any significant measures to diminish environmental pollution. They have made some efforts to conceal the gravity of the environmental problem from the general public.[37] This is aided by the general passivity of the public. A few people, concerned with the ecological situation in Zaporizhzhya, have formed a Zaporizhzhya branch of Greenpeace. Only 3 - 5 people are active in this group. In 1995 Greenpeace organised a demonstration by climbing one of the chimneys of Zaporozhstal. Ruch established an ecological group in Zaporizhzhya called 'Green Earth'. In 1994 they organised a group of people, mainly students, to come to Zaporozhstal and stay there for some days immediately under the chimneys, as a protest against pollution. The local population was symphatic and provided them with food.

With relatively cheap measures the level of emissions could be reduced significantly. It seems that the political will to improve the environmental situation is missing.

Conclusion

Zaporizhzhya is one of the most polluted towns in Ukraine and in Europe at large.

Although emission levels of pollutants have diminished since the independence of Ukraine, due to the fact that industry is producing on average at about one-third of its capacity, pollution levels are still very high and damaging for the health of the population. Even water quality has deteriorated.

The serious environmental situation asks for urgent measures as it has a very negative impact upon the health of the population. However, the public authorities have up to now not shown a willingness to undertake serious action.

Notes

1. During an international environmental conference in Krivoi Rog, April 1994, Zaporizhzhya has been mentioned as the third most polluted town in Ukraine (*Mik*, 16 April 1994).

2. Amongst these emissions there was 50,400 tonnes of dust and 218,385 tonnes of gases. Amongst the gases were 88,764 tonnes SO_2, 91,589 tonnes CO and 32,010 tonnes NO. Among 54 Ukrainian towns monitored on atmospheric air pollution, most polluted towns were in Donetsk-Pridniprovsky area; Zaporizhzhya belonged to the 13 most polluted towns (Ministry of Environment).
3. Ministry of Environment, p. 351.
4. Sieburger. The Trade and Development Agency provided partial funding (500,000 dollars) for a study of upgrading of environmental control and automation of Zaporizhzhya Aluminium Enterprise.
5. *Zaporozhka Sitch*, 28 December 1994.
6. Zaporozhkoks is responsible for 70 per cent of all phenol emissions in Zaporizhzhya town, 90 per cent of carbon disulphide emissions and 60 per cent of hydrogen sulphide emissions (*Industrialnoje Zaporizhzhya*, 4 July 1994).
7. Ministry of Environment, Kiev.
8. For each tonne of ammoniac emission, the penalty was, in early 1996, 0.5 $. *Vesti*, 20 January 1996.
9. *Vesti*, 20 January 1996.
10. Ministry of Environment, Kiev.
11. *Industrialnoje Zaporizhzhya*, 21 September 1995.
12. Ibid.
13. *Ridna Priroda*, Nr 4 - 5, 1994, pp. 2 - 87.
14. *Zaporizhka Pravda*, 5 June 1993.
15. *Ridna Priroda*, Nr 4 - 5, 1994, pp. 2 - 87.
16. Ibid.
17. *Zelenii Svet*, nr. January 1991. Most large enterprises throw their waste untreated into the Dnepr. For example, Zaporozhstal threw during 1990 2600 tonnes of heavy metal dust into the Dnepr, approximately 113 kilogram nickel, 1700 kilograms of phenol and 1610 kilograms of cyanide. According to *Molod Ukraini*, 16 May 1991.
18. *Zelonii Svet*, 6 June 1995.
19. Ministry of Environment, Kiev. Bacteriological pollution of Dnepr in Zaporizhzhya exceeded the safety levels by 100 times. (*Mits,* 9 April 1994).
20. *Zaporizka Sitch*, 7 July 1992.
21. Ministry of Environment, Kiev.
22. *Ridna Priroda*, 1994. nr 4 - 5.
23. *Zaporizka Sitch*, 7 July 1992.
24. *Zaporizka Pravda*, 3 June 1995.
25. *Perekur*, 3 September 1995, p.2.
26. Unit 3 was put into operation in January 1987, the fourth January 1988, the fifth October 1989 (after the disaster in Chernobyl) (*NEI Source Book*, fourth edition).
27. Zaporizhzhya nuclear power station has hosted personnel from plants from the United States and Spain. The plant is twinned with France's Bugey plant, with

Germany's Neckarwestheim plant and with the Catawba plant in the USA. The US Trade and Development Agency, the US Department of Energy and the International Atomic Energy Agency have assisted the plant. Contracts have been signed with US, Spanish and Croatian companies. Support comes from the side of the USA, the EU, Germany, Sweden, France and the EBRD.

28. Safety improvement work at the country's nuclear power plants has essentially come to a halt because of lack of money.
29. Forty per cent in 1993.
30. *NEI source book*, fourth edition.
31. Nine events on level 2 and 15 on level 1. All the other reported events were below the safety level 1.
32. *NEI source book*, fourth edition.
33. Coopers and Lybrand, 1993. According to *Zaporizka Pravda* of 5 June 1993, the radiation norm has been exceeded 10 times.
34. See *Echo Tchernobyl v Zaporizhzhya.*
35. *Izvestia*, 10 June 1992.
36. 21 May 1994.
37. For example, the municipal authorities installed two Geiger-Muller counters in town, one on top of the supermarket Ukraine and the other in Motor Sitch, in order to inform the population about radiation levels. The counters always display values between 10 and 12 milli Roentgen per hour, which is, according to international standards, the normal radiation level. However, when the international media reported a more than normal radioactivity level in the atmosphere of Zaporizhzhya, the counters in Zaporizhzhya showed normal values.

10 Health in Zaporizhzhya

Birth and death in Zaporizhzhya

The birth rate in Zaporizhzhya province declined from 11.7 per thousand in 1991 to 8.1 per thousand in 1996.[1] The Zaporizhzhya birth rate was in 1996 one of the lowest in Europe. In 1993, the European countries with the lowest birth rates were Germany (9.8 per thousand) and Spain (9.9 per thousand).

Twenty-five per cent of couples are infertile in Zaporizhzhya. The international standard is 8 - 9 per cent The extremely high figure for Zaporizhzhya is related to the high level of environmental pollution, the very low level of care in childhood when infections affect the future reproductive functions and the high level of abortions.[2]

Mortality increased in Zaporizhzhya province from 12.4 per thousand in 1991 to 15.0 per thousand; in 1996 Zaporizhzhya had, compared with European countries, one of the highest mortality rates. For example, the mortality in the United Kingdom was 10.9, in Germany 11.0 and in Italy 7.8 in 1992.[3]

The highest mortality rates can be found in the villages of Zaporizhzhya. Whereas in 1996 one-quarter of the population live in the villages, approximately one-third of deaths were in the villages. The mortality rate in the countryside of Zaporizhzhya was 20.3 per thousand in 1996. This high rate is related to the fact that health care facilities are almost non existent in the countryside. This picture is the same for Ukraine as a whole: the death rate in rural areas was in 1992 17.6, while it was in urban areas 11.4 per 1000.[4] The discrepancy between rural and urban areas is in this respect much greater than in other Central and Eastern European countries. In most Western European countries the death rate in rural areas is lower than in urban areas.

The number of people dying from diseases related to blood circulation, among others heart infarcts, increased from 642 per 100,000 in 1990 to 859 per 100,000 in 1995 (based on the first half-year). The absolute number of deaths from accidents, intoxication and traumas increased from 2275 in 1990 to 3980 in 1995 (based on the first half-year).

The infant mortality rate in Zaporizhzhya province is rather high. In 1992 it was 15.0 and in 1996 14.4 per 1000 There are great fluctuations across the province.[5] The Kubishev district had in 1996 an infant mortality rate of 38.4 per 1000. Zaporizhzhya infant mortality rates do not differ significantly from Ukrainian figures but are far above those in Western Europe.[6]

Since the late 1980s mortality increased dramatically and the birth rate dropped steeply. As a result the population of Zaporizhzhya began to decline at an increasing speed. In 1991 the population declined by 0.07 per cent, in 1992 by 0.25 per cent and in 1996 by 0.69 per cent. Whereas in 1991 Zaporizhzhya had 884,000 inhabitants, in 1997 the town had 871,000 inhabitants, a decline of 13,000 people.

Did men suffer more than women?

Apparently, economic and social crisis affected the health of men more than that of women. While life expectancy for women remained stable, that of men dropped from 66 years in 1989 to 62.8 years in 1994 in Ukraine.

Mortality especially increased for men in the age group of 40 - 60 years.

Table 10.1 Mortality of men and women, per 1000, in various age groups, Ukraine and United Kingdom, 1993

Age		40 - 44	45 - 49	50 - 54	55 - 59
Men	Ukraine	10.9	15.1.	19.4	26.8
	UK	2.1	3.3	5.8	10.0
Women	Ukraine	3.1	4.6	6.5	10.3
	UK	1.3	2.2	3.6	6.0

Source: *Demographic Yearbook 1995*, *UN*, *pp. 484, 485*

In Ukraine as a whole there is an enormous difference between mortality between men and women. Differences are much greater in Ukraine than in Western countries (other Western countries than the UK give similar discrepancies). Only Russia surpasses Ukraine in this respect.[7]

Generally, from approximately 1970, life expectancy in Central and Eastern European countries started to decline, due to worsening health care, bad living habits and environmental problems, whereas in Western European countries, life expectancy continued to increase. In 1990, in all Western Central and Eastern European countries, life expectancy for males was lower than 71 years, whereas in all Western European countries it was higher than 71 years. In all Central and Eastern European countries, life expectancy for females was lower than 77 years, whereas it was in all Western European countries it was higher than 77 years.[8]

Sharply declining life expectancy for males may be related to the great problem men have, especially in the age category 40 - 60, with adjusting to the situation of economic crisis and unemployment (increasing stress for men is described in Chapter 8). Also, it seems that the little care men traditionally took for their health diminished even further. Higher alcohol consumption and more smoking especially contributed to their worsening health. The fact that the suicide rate among men exploded recently, while that of women remained stable points to another reaction of men to the present crisis circumstances compared to women (see the section on suicide in this chapter).

A striking phenomenon was the massive increase in the number of deaths of elderly men in leading positions. They were often the more idealistic directors, who looked after their employees, but could not cope anymore with the new situation in which they were forced to comply with compromising situations. Among this group an explosion in mortality occurred starting 1992.

Traditionally, people in Zaporizhzhya aged quickly, related to the bad environmental situation and hard working conditions. Nowadays, in the present economic crisis, this early ageing is even more pronounced.

The spread of infectious diseases

Related to rising poverty and the deteriorating health care a number of infectious diseases have recently spread in Zaporizhzhya.

There are first of all the sexually transmitted diseases like syphilis, gonorrhoea and AIDS. In 1991 there were only 18.8 cases of syphilis per 100.000 inhabitants in Zaporizhzhya province. Since that year the ratio increased to 223 in 1996. (Ukraine: 1992: 18.3; 1996: 152). This ratio is more than 50 times higher than in Western Europe and in the USA.[9] Within Ukraine, Zaporizhzhya is here one of the leaders. Although there was an explosion of gonorrhoea cases in the early 1990s, since 1994 this situation has come under control in Zaporizhzhya (189 cases per 100,000 in 1994, 89 cases in 1996). Real figures for sexually transmitted diseases are approximately several times higher than the official figures, as many people do not register and look for self-treatment by buying medicines on the market. This is also the case for AIDS which is spreading rapidly in Zaporizhzhya.

The occurrence of sexually transmitted diseases have always been an excellent barometer for the incidence of AIDS (see syphilis and gonorrhoea). According to the Statistical Yearbook of the United Nations in 1993 there were in Eastern Europe and the countries of the former Soviet Union more than 200,000 reported cases of AIDS. World-wide there were more than 16 million AIDS cases. In Ukraine there were eight reported AIDS cases in 1992. In 1993 there were ten new cases reported. The accumulated total amounted in 1995 to 75 cases. A comparison of the above mentioned figures shows the complete unreliability of Ukrainian AIDS statistics. Also in the case of Zaporizhzhya, given the explosion of sexually transmitted diseases, one may assume that an AIDS explosion is taking place.

Unpublished data of the Zaporizhzhya Statistical Office showed the first registered case of HIV infection in 1995 and 184 cases in 1996. Apparently, it was only in 1995 that health authorities got the means to detect HIV infection.

The spread of sexually transmitted diseases is related to sexual habits. Use of contraceptives is rare, partly due to the price of these products. Often, sexual intercourse among youngsters takes place under the influence of alcohol. Also, young people are generally very badly informed about sex, the conditions of procreation and sexually transmitted diseases.

Infectious diseases that have almost disappeared in the modern world have re-appeared in South-eastern Ukraine. South-eastern Ukraine accounted for almost half of cholera morbidity in Europe during 1995.[10] Tuberculosis is spreading rapidly in Zaporizhzhya, from 33 per 100,000 in 1992 to 46 in 1996.[11] Whereas in Zaporizhzhya during 1992 9.5 per 100,000 inhabitants died from tuberculosis, in 1996 this increased to 16.8 (20.3 for the first half of 1997).[12] In Ukraine diphtheria increased by 27-fold between 1990 and 1994, measles by 44 per cent. Whereas in 1992, 9 persons per 100,000 inhabitants of Zaporizhzhya died from diphtheria (in Ukraine 2.98), in 1995 this figure has increased to 11.3 (in Ukraine 10.1). In 1996 the number declined to 8 per 100,000. However, whereas in 1992 only 0.5 per cent of diphtheria patients died, in 1996 this percentage has increased to 6.4

per cent. This increase reflects the deteriorating situation in health care provision.

Alcoholism and drug addiction

Many diseases are connected with spreading misery and poverty. Desperation pushes many to alcohol and drug abuse. Excessive drinking was deeply ingrained in Russia long before 1917. More than in most other countries, alcoholism has served for Soviet men as a means to escape daily suffering. However, since the early 1980s alcohol abuse has become more widespread although during the mid-1980s, with the anti-alcohol campaign under Gorbachev, there was a temporary decline of alcoholism.

Although according to the statistical office in Zaporizhzhya chronic alcoholism did not increase recently (140.6 new cases per 100,000 persons in 1992, 139.5 new cases in 1995; about the same level as in Ukraine as a whole), the number of alcoholics treated in hospital remained on a very high level (24,789 in 1985, 30,520 in 1990, 28,441 in 1996). Cases of alcohol psychosis sharply increased in Zaporizhzhya (from 1.94 per 10,000 in 1991 to 4.22 in 1996). Deaths from alcohol intoxication increased in Zaporizhzhya province from 271 in 1992 to 410 in 1996.

Drug addiction rose in Zaporizhzhya more sharply than in Ukraine in general, from 6 per 10,000 in 1992 to 15.43 in 1996. But only one out of ten drug addicts is registered. Deaths from drug abuse increased in Zaporizhzhya province from 16 in 1992 to 74 in 1995. The figure for 1996 is 42.

There is a well-developed drugs market, dominated by the local gypsy community. The most frequently used drugs are poppy and cannabis.

The provincial administration has set up a programme to help drug addicts. There is also a special hospital for drug addicts.

The number of fatal accidents increased tremendously in Zaporizhzhya. Whereas there were in 1988 only 686 persons died in accidents, in 1991 it increased to 1161 and in 1993 to 1232. [13]

Suicide

The suicide rate among men exploded in Zaporizhzhya (from 456 cases in Zaporizhzhya province in 1992 to 878 cases in 1996) while suicide among women remained stable (198 cases in 1992 and 162 cases in 1995). In the period 1990 to the first half of 1997 the suicide rate has increased from 23 per 100,000 to 42.4 per 100,000. In 1996, Zaporizhzhya surpassed Hungary, the European country with traditionally the highest suicide rate (38.6 in 1995).[14] The situation is even more dramatic than these figures suggest, as, for example, deaths by alcohol intoxication (271 cases in 1992, 410 cases in 1996) can often be considered as suicide although not registered in the statistics as such.

Everybody in Zaporizhzhya knows cases of suicide related to deteriorating economic and social circumstances. For example, when the house of a man was been sold to a private landlord, he had to leave his apartment. For a while he lived in the hall of the house, then neighbours forced him to move to the hall of the upper floor. He ended by throwing himself from the multi-storied house.

Environmental pollution and health

A lot of diseases and deaths occurring in Zaporizhzhya can be related to the catastrophic environmental situation. For the period 1982 - 1992 among children in Zaporizhzhya, illnesses of the upper respiratory tract occurred 45 per cent more than the average in Ukraine (correlated with phenol pollution), lung diseases occurred 91 per cent more, mouth illnesses 35 per cent, eye illnesses 35 per cent, diseases of the blood and blood organs 45 per cent more and intestinal diseases 45 per cent more. In adults cancer occurred in Zaporizhzhya town 40 per cent more than in Ukrainian towns on average and respiratory diseases 27 per cent more often (1982 - 1992).[15] Death of newborn babies, up to the age of one, was in Zaporizhzhya 10 per cent higher than in Ukraine as a whole (1982 - 1992).

Recently, morbidity has increased, especially from those diseases related to environmental pollution.

Whereas in 1988, in Zaporizhzhya town, 129 persons died from diseases of the blood and blood organs, the average for the period 1992 - 1996 was 215. Whereas in 1988 55 persons died from diseases of the digestive organs, the average for the period 1992 - 1996 was 80. In 1988, 308 persons died from breast cancer, in 1996 393 persons.

The 25 per cent infertility rate in Zaporizhzhya may also be related to the bad environmental situation.

In 1995 it was reported in Zaporizhzhya that the hospitalisation of every third person can be related to environmental pollution.[16] Diseases related to environmental pollution are above all correlated with pollution of drinking water.

Generally morbidity sharply increased in Zaporizhzhya during the last decade. This is related to bad nutrition and increased stress but also to the bad environmental situation. This is reflected in the increased occurence of non-infectious pathologies, malignant tumours and the diseases of the blood circulation and the blood itself and pregnancy pathologies. These diseases occur throughout Ukraine but above all in the industrial regions. In the whole of Ukraine birth abnormalities increased by 10 per cent in the period 1985 - 1992. Doctors in Zaporizhzhya report an even sharper increase in Zaporizhzhya.

Conclusion

Since the early 1990s the population of Zaporizhzhya is diminishing at an increasing speed. Compared to European countries, the birth rate in Zaporizhzhya is one of the lowest while the death rate is one of the highest, especially among men from age 40 to 60. Deaths from all kind of infectious diseases increased dramatically. An explosion of sexually transmitted diseases is taking place. Alcohol and drugs abuse is spreading. The suicide rate of males has attained the highest level in Europe, reflecting spreading desperation among the population.

Although atmospheric pollution has diminished, due to industrial decline, the level of general environmental pollution has not diminished. Morbidity, related to environmental pollution, has increased sharply since 1990. The hospitalisation of every third person in Zaporizhzhya can be attributed to environmental pollution.

Notes

1. The birth rate for Ukraine was in 1991: 13.0; in 1996: 9.1.
2. Recently, the number of abortions increased. In Ukraine, for every 100 births there are 153 abortions, *Demographic Yearbook 1994*, UN, p. 323.
3. *Demographic Yearbook 1994*, UN.
4. *Demographic Yearbook 1994*, UN, pp. 409, 410.

5. The mortality of babies in their first year has dropped considerably in Zaporizhzhya province, from 15.88 per 1000 in 1991 to 11.59 per 1000 in 1996. The mortality of babies just after birth dropped from 7.94 per 1000 in 1991 to 5.31 per 1000 in 1996.
6. Infant mortality rates were for Ukraine in 1990 13.0 and for 1995 15.0. Infant death rates were for the years 1990 and 1994 for Russia 26.9 and 23.4, for Poland 16.0 and 15.1, for Italy 8.6 and 6.7, for The Netherlands 7.1 and 5.9 and for Germany 7.1 and 5.8 (*Demographic Yearbook 1994,* UN, p. 378, *World Development Indicators*, 1997).
7. Mortality among Russian men of 40 - 49 years was 16.3 per 1000 in 1995, whereas it was 9.2 in 1990 (*International Herald Tribune*, 9 June 1997).
8. Coleman, p. 128.
9. *International Herald Tribune*, 19 May 1997. The incidence of syphilis in Western Europe dropped to below 2 per 100,000. The countries of the former Soviet Union have experienced a dramatic increase in syphilis from 5 per 100,000 in 1990 to 170 per 100,000 in 1995 (*Economist*, 17 May 1997, p. 58).
10. *Human Development Report*, UN, 1996.
11. The tuberculosis rate in Ukraine was in 1992 35, in 1994 39.9.
12. In 1996, in Ukraine 14 per 100,000 died from tuberculosis.
13. *Zaporizka Sitch* 3 November 1994.
14. In 1992, the highest suicide rate in Europe were recorded by Estonia (38.2), Russia (37.3) and Hungary (35.9). Austria, traditionally, with Hungary, scoring high, had a rate of 21.2. In Germany the are was 15.6, in the United Kingdom 8.0, in Italy 7.8 and in Bulgaria, surprisingly, 7.8 (Statistical Yearbook, UN, 1993).
15. Tokarenko, Ivanov.
16. *Industrialnoje Zaporizhzhya*, 4 July 1995.

11 A Rapidly Changing World

Development in isolation

One of the major changes in Zaporizhzhya since 1985, the advent of Gorbachev to power, has been the gradual opening-up of society and the economy. Up to that time Zaporizhzhya developed in isolation from the world outside the former Soviet Union and tsarist Russia. With Perestroika there were more opportunities to become informed about world events and to develop international links. However, despite this process, by the late 1990s, Zaporizhzhya was still to a large extent a closed society. A foreign visitor will notice that very few people in Zaporizhzhya are able to speak a foreign language, that there is no tourist infrastructure and that it is not possible to buy any serious literature in foreign languages other than Russian. Ukrainian newspapers, especially the local ones, hardly inform about the world outside the former Soviet Union and travelling abroad is a prerogative for the few. Although Zaporizhzhya has almost one million inhabitants it gives the impression of an inward-looking provincial town with a very low level of cultural infrastructure.

Internationalisation processes have had up to now only a limited impact upon Zaporizhzhya society. Generally, people do not have the money to travel abroad. Students do not have the means to inform themselves about the world. Libraries stock hardly any periodicals and books in foreign languages other than Russian. Students in economics have to learn about market economies through Russian and Ukrainian translations of mainly English and American textbooks. Travelling abroad is very expensive. An international passport, that most Zaporizhzhya citizens do not have, costs 100 dollars. Obtaining a visa for a Western country is very complicated and expensive. Travelling abroad in most cases means coach travels to countries like Poland, Slovakia and Germany, to trade products for the Zaporizhzhya bazaars. For many this travelling has become a major source of income. The bazaar is flooded with foreign products.

Although in some respects one can speak about an opening towards the world in recent years, reverse trends are also discernible. Links with Moscow and St Petersburg, the major cultural and scientific centres in the former Soviet Union, have weakened very much. Also, cultural and scientific exchange has diminished drastically. For example, in Soviet times, there would be many students from the Third World in Zaporizhzhya, studying in Zaporizhzhya under the framework of inter-state agreements. Since independence of Ukraine this number has dropped dramatically. Nowadays, about 1000 foreign students remain. Life has been made very difficult for these students as universities and academies try to squeeze these students financially, without rendering adequate services in return.

The disruption of supply chains

With the collapse of the Soviet Union, many of the supply chains, especially for the all-Union enterprises, were severed and new suppliers had to be found in Ukraine (see also Chapter 3). This appeared to be rather difficult and was hampered by the lack of horizontal communication and the lack of databases. In some cases the provincial administration helped.[1]

In the period 1991 - 1994, the decline of trade with Russia was moderate, compared with the period 1994 - 1997. Whereas in 1994 the countries of the former Soviet Union still accounted for 68 per cent of total exports, in 1996 this percentage has declined to 36 per cent. In the first phase of independence trade links with Russia were primarily hampered by the chaos arising from the collapse of the centrally planned economy. In 1993 a free-trade zone was announced within the Community of Independent States to which Ukraine belonged. However, since then trade barriers were erected and at the end of 1996 President Kuchma spoke about economic warfare after Russia announced the levying of a 20 per cent tax upon imports originating from Ukraine; Ukraine subsequently did the same with imports from Russia. In the period 1991 - 1994 it was usually a problem to find suppliers, since then the problem, in trade with other countries of the former Soviet Union, is to pay for supplies.

It is not only trade barriers that led Zaporizhzhya enterprises to dismiss Russian suppliers and look for suppliers elsewhere. Russian suppliers, in many cases, have become too expensive, compared to potential suppliers in Central and Western Europe (see the example of Avtozaz in Chapter 5).

Supply chains were also disrupted in another manner. The opportunity to trade abroad led many enterprises to break former relations with Ukrainian clients and suppliers. This has often led to the disruption of whole supply chains.

A typical example is the following: a Zaporizhzhya factory has been very successful in exporting leather jackets to the West. However, it became more profitable for the local leather supplier to export leather to the West. The leather jacket manufacturer went bankrupt as a consequence. Subsequently the slaughterhouse found it more profitable to export raw unprocessed leather than to supply the local leather manufacturer. The leather manufacturer went banktrupt. Subsequently agriculture fell into a deep crisis and cattle breeders found it more profitable to export live cattle abroad than to supply the local slaughterhouse. The slaughterhouse went bankrupt.[2]

This is an example of how new export opportunities can disrupt existing supply chains. More often, import competition may led to the disruption of supply chains. In the joint ventures visited, we have noticed that, in order to guarantee quality, suppliers had to be sought abroad. Ukrainian suppliers could, in most cases, not deliver products of the required quality.[3]

The fact that the prices of Ukrainian enterprises are often too high is also related to a peculiar price-setting rule that only applies for domestic trade. This rule is called the principle of cost-covering prices, that is, the factory should take into account in the price the costs of letting the enterprise produce from the moment onward that production has halted for the last client. This means, for example, that if a factory has not produced for three months and starts production for a new client, this client has to pay for the three months that the factory has not worked.[4] This is an odd rule, but forces enterprises to set high prices for Ukrainian clients. It has the result that steel prices for Ukrainian consumers are 30 - 50 per cent higher than for foreign clients. This system of price setting contributes to a continuing depression in domestic markets and pushes Ukrainian enterprises to seek foreign producers.The bad debt chain also induces Ukrainian enterprises to set higher prices and more strict delivery conditions for Ukrainian markets.

Disruption of supply chains also occurred in Central European countries. However, due to the slow pace of transition in Ukraine, the relatively high production costs in Ukraine and the comparatively very low quality standards, the disruption of supply chains through import competition has been in Ukraine much more drastic and poses a danger for the economy as a whole.

Import competition

With respect to final products, import competition has been severe. In the West it is argued that import competition may function as a crowbar to break domestic monopolies and to further competition with the effect of better domestic production.

Ukraine seems to be a peculiar case in the sense that adjustment to import competition has been very limited, compared to most Central European countries, due to the fact that the Ukrainian economy has been marketised only to a very limited extent. One indicator is the very low privatisation rate. The lack of response to import competition is also related to the high taxation rate and the overvalued hrivna, making it very difficult for domestic producers to compete. The result is that imports are encouraged and exports discouraged. All these factors led to the situation where import competition is killing rather than stimulating domestic producers.

The disastrous impact of import competition is related to the slow pace of reform, rather than assumed unfair competition.[5]

For example, the provincial administration of Zaporizhzhya imported a large quantity of Dutch butter that appeared to be one and a half times cheaper than locally produced butter.[6] Paradoxically, the kolkhozes hardly get an adequate price for their products.

Many food products from Western Europe are offered at the Zaporizhzhya markets, of a better quality and lower price than local food products. This runs against any economic theory.

Also labour-intensive products from Western Europe can compete with local products in Zaporizhzhya markets. While economic text books teach us that countries like Ukraine, have a huge comparative advantage in these products.

With respect to price and quality of labour, the following should be taken into account. In early 1993, the average monthly wage in industry has been in the range of 7 dollars a month. By early 1996, the average industrial wage had surpassed 100 dollars a month.[7] But, this is the net wage, not taking into account the high taxes and the indirect subsidies of government and enterprises to employees. A local private textile factory, mainly producing for the domestic market, had to pay its employees salaries in the range of 50 - 80 dollars. This is a branch with a relatively low wage level, about 35 dollar per month. This means that in order to become competitive, the private factory had to pay about twice the average salary in the branch.

And again, taxes are not taken into account. Of course, wages remain low, but not as low as the statistical office would let us believe.

Then there is a problem in the quality of labour. Despite the relatively high education level of the population, the average quality of the labour force is rather poor. Low average productivity is not only related to the way labour is organised, but also related to deeply ingrained attitudes. The labour productivity of a private firm, in which the management tries to organise labour in a modern way, does not always lead to similar productivity levels as in the West because the average labour productivity is held down by the general economic environment and deeply rooted attitudes.

Foreign economic policy of the government has been inconsistent. After a phase in which even exports were taxed, a liberalisation of foreign trade took place. However, recently, import tariffs have been raised and reached in early 1996 an average level of 25 per cent, which is high compared with average world standards.[8] On the other hand, the National Bank keeps the dollar-hrivna rate very high. For example, during 1996 inflation was 80 per cent, while the dollar-hrivna exchange rate hardly changed.

Imports and exports

In 1996, 44.2 per cent of registered Zaporizhzhya imports originated in the countries of the former Soviet Union.[9] In 1994, 73 per cent of imports used to come from the CIS region. Approximately half of all imports are not registered. Most of these imports can be found in the bazaar and are, in most cases, consumer goods and food products. They are mainly coming from the 'far abroad' and constitute a large share of actual imports.

By Ukrainian standards, Zaporizhzhya is economically a very open economy. Whereas Zaporizhzhya province only accounts for 4 per cent of the population of Ukraine, it accounted for about 7 per cent of all Ukrainian exports in 1996. Exports from Zaporizhzhya gradually increased during the first half of the 1990s. This rise was primarily based on increased exports of raw materials or semi-manufactured products. The export of iron increased from 98 million tonnes in 1991 to 1202 tonnes in 1995, the export of steel from 234 million tonnes in 1991 to 701 million tonnes in 1995 (see Table 5.1)

The structure of exports is very unfavourable. The export of heavy metals and aluminium constituted in 1996 67 per cent of all exports (48.5 per cent in 1994).

The seven largest enterprises accounted for 68 per cent of all exports in 1994. The increase in exports is related to relatively cheap inputs of the iron, steel and aluminium exporters, low amortisation rates, very low expenditure of funds for environment concerns, cheap credits and other hidden subventions by the state. This background points to the unsustainability of the present level of exports. The rise in exports up to 1996 hides the very weak export base of Zaporizhzhya region. The backlash at a later phase may be comparatively harder.

The geographical structure of export markets of Zaporizhzhya provicne recently made a radical shift in taking exports away from the former Soviet Union. Whereas in 1994 the countries of the former Soviet Union accounted for 68 per cent of total exports, in 1996 this has declined to 36 per cent (for the period before 1994 no figures are available). While exports to the countries of the former Soviet Union have remained on the same level, the exports to the 'far abroad', that is countries outside the former Soviet Union, have increased tremendously.

The share of exports to Central and Eastern European countries, outside the former Soviet Union, fluctuated between 6 and 10 per cent during 1994 - 1997. The share of China increased from 8.6 per cent in 1995 to 20 per cent in first half of 1997. The share of Germany remained very marginal (1.9 per cent in 1994, 0.9 per cent in the first half of 1997) and the USA became marginal (10.9 per cent in 1995, 1.6 per cent in the first half of 1997).[10]

Despite the large number of joint ventures, about 300, international industrial co-operation is on a rather low level. Joint ventures are mainly in commercial activities, with a low degree of interaction with the foreign partner. This low level of international co-operation is in contrast with the high level of foreign trade of Zaporizhzhya province.

This should be seen in the context of Soviet history, in which foreign economic relations were mainly confined to the sphere of trade in tangible commodities. Foreign trade used to be organised by specialised foreign trade firms in Moscow. Usually, firms did not know their clients and suppliers abroad. International technology transfer was very limited and mainly confined to the buying and copying of foreign technology. The revolution in production organisation in the most advanced market economies went largely unnoticed in the former Soviet Union, and is still hardly noticed in Zaporizhzhya. In their mental set-up, the overwhelming number of enterprise managers still seem to have a Taylorist or even pre-Taylorist conception of production organisation.

Therefore, when talking about international industrial co-operation, enterprises and administration mainly have in mind the attraction of capital and machinery and less so organisational know-how.

In interviews with enterprise management of joint ventures, it appeared that a lot of them have had problems with their foreign partners. With some it appeared that the Western partner abused the limited knowledge of legal affairs with the Ukrainian partner in order to have very cheap access to Ukrainian products and know-how.

We have observed a widespread mistrust among interviewed managers, also from joint ventures, about the aims of their Western partners. From Western businesspeople dealing with the Ukraine we have heard that their Ukrainian partners often do not respect the status of contracts and they complain about the fact that in Ukraine, a law-governed economy does not function. Foreign partners complain about the lack of respect for personal commitments as well, being late to meetings is commonplace and failure to follow through is frequent.[11]

Foreign direct investment

Despite the high level of exports, related to Gross Domestic Product, the province of Zaporizhzhya had by early 1997 the lowest level of foreign direct investment of all provinces in Ukraine.[12] Also, Ukraine has one of the lowest per capita foreign direct investment levels within Central and Eastern Europe, despite the advantage of having a potential big market.[13] In the period 1991 - 1996 42.3 billion dollars flowed into Central and Eastern Europe as net foreign direct investment. Only 1.2 billion dollars went to Ukraine. Cumulative per capita inflows amounted in Ukraine in that period to 23 dollars. Only Armenia, Georgia and Belarus had in Europe lower per capita inflows.

The low level of foreign direct investment in Ukraine is related to the bad general economic and political situation as described in Chapter 2. On top of that, regulations for foreign direct investment regularly change and sometimes the investor has to pay taxes retroactively, and penalties if the activity was not illegal when done.[14] It has happened that the president gave foreign investors a guarantee removing the obligation to pay taxes to gain investments, while at the same time the parliament adopted a law that obliges foreign investors to pay taxes. Generally, this legal confusion is frightening foreign investors.

At first sight, Zaporizhzhya has done a lot to attract foreign direct investment. It is the first province in Ukraine to make a regional development plan, for which it has invited the consultant firm Coopers and Lybrand, and a for a lot of enterprises business plans have been made. A seminar about foreign direct investment was held in December 1995, Zaporizhzhya presented itself in the annual fair in Hanover in April 1996, and some institutions have been established to attract foreign direct investment.[15]

However, few concrete steps have been made to make Zaporizhzhya more attractive for foreign investors. Local authorities still cannot tell a foreign investor how much time it will take to arrange land and communication infrastructure. There is almost no information that can be obtained about Zaporizhzhya by foreign investors. A negative factor for Zaporizhzhya is the relatively poor communication and public transport infrastructure and the bad environmental situation.

Most foreign direct investment came from Canada (3.6 million doliars), Virgin Islands (2.6 million dollars), USA (1.7 million dollars), China (0.8 million dollars) and Germany (0.5 million dollars) (as of 1 July 1996).[16]

It remains to be seen, however, to what extent the announced investment of Daewoo in Avtozaz may change the general economic climate in Zaporzhzhia.

The internationalisation processes

The low level of industrial co-operation and foreign direct investment is directly related to the low level of internationalisation of Zaporizhzhya society and economy. Very few people travel abroad and few foreigners visit Zaporizhzhya.

A general problem with international co-operation is that local businessmen, especially older ones, do not have any idea how to behave with respect to foreign partners. The isolation of Zaporizhzhya prevented many from learning about how to behave in international business circles. Generally, they lack general civilised behaviour, they have the wrong expectations about business partners, do not value the role of contracts in economic transactions and often do not respect agreements.[17]

To attract foreigners it is important to enhance the service infrastructure, for example, Western standard hotel accomodation, at reasonable prices.

Foreign assistance

During the 1990s Zaporizhzhya began to profit from assistance projects financed by Western donors. Lecturers from European Union countries and the United States came to Zaporizhzhya in order to teach languages, computer science and economics. Researchers from Zaporizhzhya began to co-operate with partners from Western countries. In the framework of the TACIS assistance programme of the European Union, a project came into being to support sunflower growing co-operatives, with the assistance of French experts. A Business Communication Centre was established with European Union TACIS money. The Zaporizhzhya Chamber of Commerce got assistance as well as the Regional Development Agency. Coopers and Lybrand compiled for the provincial administration a report about regional development prospects, with Western money. A lot of enterprises made a business plan, with assistance from Western sources. The nuclear power plant got help from Western experts. The EurAsia Foundation had several projects in Zaporizhzhya. This list could easily be enlarged with other examples. Germany especially showed interest in the development of Zaporizhzhya and Zaporizhzhya was selected as one of the three Ukrainian provinces where most German assistance should be directed.

Experiences with assistance projects are mixed. Generally, local and provincial authorities were only interested in Western money, not in advice. The provincial adminisatration did practically nothing with the advice of Coopers and Lybrand, that had cost 750,000 dollars. The report became classified material. The only tangible result was the establishment of a regional development centre. However, this centre did not do anything.

Usually, the running of projects financed by Western donors is crucially dependent on the presence of Western advisors. Once the Western advisors left the well-equipped Business Communication Centre, its activities slowed down.

Often, there were cases of corruption in relation with respect to Western assistance projects. In most cases, local and regional authorities were not co-operative with Western advisors.

For example, when a French team came to Zaporizhzhya for the TACIS- financed sunflower project, the responsible functionaries in the provincial administration did not offer any help to the experts. They offered to mediate for the delivery of office and office equipment, including secretarial aid, for an astronomical amount of money. The firm Hortitsa would take care of that. It was obvious that there was a deal between the respective functionaries in the provincial administration and Hortitsa to financially squeeze the TACIS experts. Subsequently, with great efforts, the French consultants found office space themselves.

Repeatedly, Western money destined for researchers in Zaporizhzhya has been appropriated by the leadership of academies and universities. When a researcher from the Technical University of Zaporizhzhya managed to obtain funds from the United States to conduct a research project, she never saw the money the vice-rector had appropriated.

Many more cases of corruption with respect to Western assistance money are known.

Conclusion

Despite new opportunities to travel abroad and to inform about the outside world, Zaporizhzhya remained a closed and provincial society. The internationalisation of Zaporizhzhya society and economy remained on a very low level. It was mainly an internationalisation of the bazaar that took place. Although Zaporizhzhya exports attained a high level, by Ukrainian standards, these exports have a fragile basis as they are, for the larger part, subsidised. Foreign direct investment and international industrial co-operation is at a very low level, also according to Ukrainian standards. Import competition killed Zaporizhzhya enterprises rather than stimulating them to perform better.

Generally, Western assistance projects have encountered numerous obstacles, among which is the unco-operative attitude of local and regional authorities and widespread corruption.

Notes

1. Such as in the case of inter-regional cooperation in South-east Ukraine where supplies of coal for Zaporizhzhya enterprises have been secured.
2. The example is from Professor Niethammer, who did research in Zaporizhzhya.
3. For example, ZTL company in Zaporizhzhya imports from Hungary a fruit concentrate for making lemonade. The Hungarian concentrate has a shelf-life of one year while Ukrainian concentrate keeps only one month. Bolshoi Kazachok exports feathers to Germany where they are cleaned and sorted. Subsequently they are re-imported to be processed for duvets. A factory in Kyiv, that has the equipment to do the same job, can not attain the required quality.

4. Hirschhausen, p. 7.
5. Although there is unfair import competition. Many imports enter the country illegally, without any import tax. For example, VEPES textile factory complained about the selling of cheap Turkish textiles, which were not taxed at all, either in Turkey or at Ukrainian borders.
6. *Delovaya Ukraina*, 15 November 1995, p. 12.
7. In December 1995, the average wage in Zaporizhzhya industry has been 16,825,000 karbonavets a month (Zaporizke 1996a, p. 129). With an exchange rate of 187,000 karbonavets for one dollar this makes 90 dollar per month. In March 1996 the average monthly wage has surpassed the 100-dollar barrier. This rise in wage level is only related to the karbonavets-dollar exchange rate.
8. *Zerkalo Nedeli*. 17 February 1996, p. 7.
9. Zaporizke 1997a.
10. Zaporizke 1997a, p. 70.
11. Information obtained at the annual conference of the Utrecht Chamber of Commerce about Ukraine, in which about 80 Dutch entrepreneurs participated.
12. As of 1 July 1995, Zaporizhzhya had attracted 1.5 per cent of all foreign direct investment in Ukraine. Zaporizhzhya accounts for 4 per cent of Ukrainian population (*Ukraina ta ii regioni*).
13. Per capita cumulative inflow of foreign direct investment during the period 1991 - 1996 was 21 dollars in Ukraine, 66 dollars in Romania, 5 dollars in Belarus, 32 dollars in Russia, 1,198 dollars in Hungary, 586 dollars in Czech Republic and 121 dollars in Poland.
14. In the five years since independence, legal conditions for FDI changed six times in Ukraine (*Ekonomika Ukraini*, January 1997, p. 37).
15. Chamber of Industry and Commerce, Regional Development Agency and Business Communication Center.
16. Zaporizhzhya Statistical Office. A lot of investment comes from tax havens such as the Virgin Islands (2.6 million dollars), Hungary (292,000 dollars), Cyprus (292,000 dollars), Bahamas (138,000 dollars), Liechtenstein (115,000 dollars) and Lebanon (100,000 dollars). Most probably, it is black market money from Zaporizhzhya, whitewashed through these tax paradises.
17. A Turkish businessman told us how Zaporozhstal regularly did not deliver steel on the agreed-upon date, so that the Turkish trader got into difficulties with his clients about the contractual delivery date. The enterprise leadership did not understand that such behaviour inflicts penalties upon the Turkish trader. As a result payment for deliveries is nowadays at the moment of shipment of steel.

Conclusion

This book has analysed the major changes in the society and economy of Zaporizhzhya since Perestroika accelerated the disintegration of Soviet communism. These changes are often summarised, as for the rest of Central and Eastern Europe, as the change-over from a centrally planned to a market economy and from party dictatorship to parliamentary democracy. However, Zaporizhzhya, that may be considered as representative for the many industrial centres in the former Soviet Union, shows that transition is not a teleological process that automatically leads to some form of market economy and a parliamentary democracy.

The new socio-economic system has not yet stabilised, but what emerges looks more like a kleptocracy, with feudal traits, that has retained many elements from the communist and tsarist past, than like a modern market economy. Parliamentary democracy is mainly a facade for the continuation of the rule of the old Nomenklature, clinging to secrecy and authoritarian rule. However, party discipline has been replaced by clan loyalty and a system of mutual dependencies in which no one of the ruling elite can afford to flout. New economic laws allowed the private appropriation of state property, without, however, creating capitalism. Economic 'liberalisation' created capitalists without capitalism. The emerging socio-economic system is not producing new wealth but geared towards the redistribution of existing, and declining wealth.

The redistributive syndrome, channelling funds towards big loss-making enterprises, is too heavy a burden for the few healthy enterprises. Therefore, the economic base of Zaporizhzhya is eroding quickly. The industrial base of Zaporizhzhya has collapsed and by early 1998 there were no signs that market economy had attained a critical mass or that new economic sectors might replace the role of the old large industrial enterprises. The metallurgical enterprises mainly survive by exporting. However, their competitiveness is based on hidden subsidies. Once these subsidies are taken away, they will not be able to compete anymore, which will lead to further industrial decline.

Import competition is killing industrial enterprises in Zaporizhzhya rather than stimulating their competitiveness. The Ukrainian government does not provide a favourable legal context for economic development in Zaporizhzhya. Laws are contradictory and prevent industrial development from taking place. Distrust in public life and lawlessness favour those forces that prefer to earn money by trading or stealing.

History matters, as the persistence of old behavioural routines and perseverance of traditional norms and values show. It seems that the reflexes created under tsarism and communism and that proved to be adequate to survive under these dictatorships, are counter-productive in the new circumstances. For example, while initiative was hitherto always punished, it is now crucial for survival. However, in Zaporizhzhya society, old reflexes, that have created a mutual enforcing system of negative feedbacks, are quite persistent and constitute a major barrier for social and economic development.

There are many persistent attitudes from communist times that form an obstacle to modern economic development. There is the inclination to keep information for oneself and the aversion to co-operation and openness. There is the tendency to cheat and lie in public life that contributes to the general distrust in economic life. No one respects contracts or the law. Corruption has become a way of life. All this enhances transaction costs enormously.

One can say that the social conditions necessary for modern economic development are nowadays absent in Zaporizhzhya.

The social context in which the population lives has changed drastically. In Soviet times the state took care of citizens from birth to death. Nowadays this care system is complete absent with the collapse of all kinds of social services. There has been a change-over from excessive social control to jungle individualism. This, together with widespread poverty, has driven people into a despair that is reflected in the highest suicide rate in Europe, excessive consumption of alcohol and the spread of drug addiction.

Young people can best cope with the new situation, but this is accompanied by negative phenomena like the spread of juvenile delinquency and the mentality that everything should be paid for. Middle-aged men seem to be the most vulnerable group as the mortality rate among them has increased enormously. Generally, the mortality rate had increased sharply and already surpassed the birth rate in 1991 with the result that the population of Zaporizhzhya is declining at an increasing speed. The birth rate in Zaporizhzhya is one of the lowest in Europe, while the death rate is one of the highest in Europe.

Relations between the genders have become increasingly under strain with economic hardships. In public life women became even more marginalised. However, the role of women as the backbone of the private sphere became even more pronounced.

The main event for the general population since the independence of Ukraine is that the majority of the population has been thrown into deep poverty. They usually survive by retreating to the most primitive forms of economy, by intensifying the cultivation of gardens and extending the network of services among friends.

The disintegration of the old social system with the concomitant falling-away of such external disciplining forces as the party, as well as the increasing strain on family life has enabled the emergence of numerous problems among young people.

A moral vacuum and lawlessness in society have contributed to a crime explosion in society. The murder rate in Zaporizhzhya has surpassed that of almost all European countries.

The well-being of future generations is jeopardised by the rapid breakdown of all kinds of public services. What previous generations had built up over decades is now being broken down in the course of one decade. The breakdown of the social and physical infrastructure presents an enormous burden for future generations

The de-industrialisation of Zaporizhzhya and that of South-eastern Ukraine at large, is unprecedented in European history. The place of Zaporizhzhya changed, in a historically very short period, from one of the main industrial centres of one of the two world superpowers, towards a declining peripheral region in the wider European space, as part of a new country that found itself in the margin of European politics.

Moreover, the Ukrainisation of Ukraine meant for Zaporizhzhya a break of old historical ties with Russia. Moscow had always been the major point of orientation for Zaporizhzhya citizens, who are in the majority Russian speaking. The Ukrainisation campaign contributed to a marginalisation of Russian culture and world culture as such.

Although transition to a new economic system also meant a gradual opening-up of the economy, i.e. more foreign trade with the world outside the former Soviet Union, some foreign direct investment and numerous co-operative links with foreign firms, Zaporizhzhya remained very provincial and in many ways cut off from world economy and society.

However, this isolation will be temporary as globalisation processes will open up Zaporizhzhya even further. The question is how Zaporizhzhya will cope with the challenges world society and world economy will pose.

Certain development paths will be highly unlikely for Zaporizhzhya given the constraints of a set of structurally inhibiting factors, like the existence of a predatory ruling elite in Zaporizhzhya, a suffocating bureaucracy, bad government on the national level, lawlessness and widespread corruption. Given the inertia of value systems, it is unlikely that civil society will develop rapidly, to enable a democratic scenario to take place. It seems unlikely that the traditional industrial base will be revitalised as decay has gone too far and needed huge investments will not be available in the foreseeable future. The announced investment of Daewoo does not change much in this respect.

In a more positive scenario, if local, regional and national authorities allow it to happen, small and medium-sized enterprises may flourish, capitalising on cheap labour and available skills, finding new markets abroad. The agro-industrial complex and consumer goods industry have especially good development chances.

A threat for the immediate future is that, given the deepening financial crisis of the state, the disfunctioning economic system and exhaustion of available resources, the living standards of the majority of the population will decline to such an extent that widespread undernutrition and epidemics will occur. Also, further impoverishment of the masses may provoke social unrest and political instability.

Appendix 1

The Stalinist Socio-psychological Syndrome

Hans van Zon

In this appendix one of the authors of this book describes his personal experiences with citizens of Zaporizhzhya. His observations with regard to the set of attitudes and behavioural patterns to be found in Zaporizhzhya provides an essential contribution to an understanding of the general situation of Zaporizhzhya today.

Whereas many observers of the former Soviet Union share the view that attitudes rooted in the Soviet and Tsarist past constitute an important obstacle to social and economic progress, hardly any systematic analysis has been made of what can be characterised as the Stalinist socio-psychological syndrome.[1] Here it is suggested that Stalinist rule, and more broadly, the communist and tsarist past, has produced a system of values, norms and behavioural patterns that is quite persistent and that is able to replicate itself. The syndrome is labelled 'Stalinist' as the syndrome was perfected under Stalin and can be best explained with regard to the Stalinist socio-economic system. Some of its traits have been preserved since then, even when the party-state on which this system was built had collapsed.

This Stalinist socio-psychological syndrome will be described below. Emphasis will be placed on the interrelationships between its component parts and reference will continuously be made to personal experiences in Zaporizhzhya. Since this phenomenon has hardly been systematically analysed, there will be few references to literature.

The cult of power

Although parliamentary democracy has been formally introduced, the political system and society at large is still very much authoritarian in Zaporizhzhya (see Chapter 4). Power in Zaporizhzhya is generally not countervailed. Bureaucrats and enterprise directors reign in their domains as absolutist monarchs. It is normal for the rector of a higher education institute to ask a subordinate lecturer to paint his house. An enterprise director can fire an employee whenever he wants. Exercise of power in Zaporizhzhya has absolutist traits as power in Zaporizhzhya always has been, in Soviet and in tsarist times, absolutist. There is no tradition of challenging power because this has been severely punished in the past. Asking people in Zaporizhzhya why they tolerate unbearable circumstances at their workplace or in their town, the usual answer is: the choice is between slavery and dismissal, or between slavery and civil war. For Zaporizhzhya there seems not to exist a third way, that of civil disobedience.

Power is exercised in an absolutist and arbitrary way and this is reinforced by the way the ruled react. It is not to say that the people of Zaporizhzhya are to be blamed for the way they are governed. But the way power relations are reproduced in Zaporizhzhya is partially rooted in the acceptance or tolerance by the subject people.

Absolutist power and the totalitarian power of the communist party-state created a cult of power. The attribute of power became so overwhelmingly important in the totalitarian state where almost everything was subordinated to the will of the central power that power, and therewith the lack of it, became of overriding importance in everyday life.

Absolutist and totalitarian power meant that those in power wanted to control as much as possible the behaviour of their subordinates. A control mania is visible in all spheres of life. There is, for example, the teacher who has to supply to the authorities a detailed account of the themes he or she wants to discuss in each lesson, or, civil servants who want to make life for citizens as difficult as possible through absurd rules.

A telling example is that of a German who worked in Zaporizhzhya. He sent a report to his parent firm in Germany. He got the report back with an accompanying letter from a customs officer: asking for translation of the report into Russian! Customs officers often open letters destined for addressees in Ukraine. It is forbidden to send credit cards or cheques from abroad to residents in Ukraine. [2]

Citizens are not protected by law, even though there may be some laws that are intended to protect people. Ukraine is a lawless society where the law does not function and where breaking the law does, in principle, not necessarily have consequences. For example, a bakery in Zaporizhzhya, a joint venture with an American company, one day was taken over by a gang. The municipality and police did nothing and the bakery, although it stopped producing, is still in the hands of the Mafia gang.

The availability of absolutist power generates the desire to use this power by those who exercise it. It is visible in the functionaries of the town and provincial administration who are usually quite rude towards their clients. I was regularly faced with this rudeness, although this rudeness is certainly less with regard to foreigners. More often than not, these functionaries did not keep their promises with regard to me as far as enterprise visits or appointments were concerned. It is the powerlessness of the individuals faced with absolutist power that nurtured the rudeness of officials. It generally furthers the contempt of the feelings of indivuals and the rights of individuals.

A Dane was once stopped by the Zaporizhzhya police. They threatened to confiscate his car because he did not have a fire extinguisher. It was only when the visiting card of the chairman of the provincial council was shown that the policeman withdrew his threat. Almost all Ukrainian citizens are helpless with regard to such abuse of power.

Due to the nature of power as is exercised in Zaporizhzhya the very notion of power as such, and politics in general, becomes discredited. Power is not used to facilitate but rather to block initiatives coming from below. The usual attitude of bosses in Zaporizhzhya is that everything that happens in their domain should be controlled by them. Independent initiatives are incompatible with such an attitude. It means that exercise of power in Zaporizhzhya is usually paralysing.

At the same time there is a refusal to delegate power. The following example is illustrative: I had to organise a small competition in Zaporizhzhya in order to get a team of researchers to participate in a research project. I asked the international department of the university to provide me with three researchers from the university who might participate in the competition. The university would gain a year's salary for each of the three researchers. I gave them approximately ten days to find a team. On the last day I was told that no team could be formed since the rector was absent and no decision about a team could be made because the rector decides everything.

It was the above described cult of power that enabled people in power on all levels to abuse their positions during the transition to a 'market economy' in order to appropriate state property on a massive scale.

Power is not intended to be used in a constructive way, although in communist times there was a typical developmental ideology that helped the Soviet economy to increase production. However, it is remarkable that with the collapse of the party-state, old communists, who usually stayed in power, suddenly let their 'developmental' face drop and lost every interest in the common good. Apparently, this developmental facade was imposed by the party and not internalised by many communist bosses.

Generally, the impression I have after numerous interviews with people within the ruling elite of Zaporizhzhya, both political and economic leaders, is that most of them are not at all interested in the social and economic development of Zaporizhzhya. This impression is confirmed by well-informed people in Zaporizhzhya, Ukrainian citizens as well as foreigners. Power is seen as an aim in itself. This contributed to the changeover from extreme community spirit and social control towards a kind of jungle individualism.

Because of the way power is exercised and the long history of absolutist power, people have generally become very compliant and accept almost everything that is imposed on them. Therefore Zaporizhzhya, and Ukraine at large, can be ruled with impunity. Rulers hardly have to take the general interest into account.

The following example of compliance is showing: in the autumn of 1995 a general one-day strike had been organised by the trade unions in Ukraine. In order to show his loyalty to the authorities, the director of Avtozaz, the local car manufacturer, had during the weekend approached all his employees, ordering them to come to the factory, although the factory had not worked for several weeks due to lack of orders. Also, the factory had wage payment arrears. Nevertheless, all employees turned up on Monday, the day of the general strike.

It is peculiar to Zaporizhzhya that the people who are faced with delays in payment of salary of up to 6 months, continue to work. No action has been undertaken against this payment delay. Striking is made difficult as the local authorities have to give permission. Striking without permission means being dismissed.

Related to the cult of power is the general mistrust in public life. In Soviet times people were taught not to speak the truth in public and they were asked to repeat lies prepared by public authorities. This background explains partly the present mistrust in public life and the widespread cheating in business. It is the lack of trust that constitutes one of the major obstacles to economic development.[3]

Totalitarian power and oppression deterred trust and the development of horizontal cooperation networks in society. Zaporizhzhya society is still very much atomised. Only the small circle of family and friends can be trusted.[4] Zaporizhzhya society can be considered as a conglomerate of thousands of small groups of families and clans that hardly communicate with one another.

This explains the very limited knowledge most inhabitants have about their own society. Sharing knowledge with people who do not belong to the same clan is not common.

The culture of dependence and reluctance to assume responsibility

The cult of power, typical in all countries that belonged to the former Soviet Union, with the possible exception of the Baltic states, has led to a culture of dependence. Independent behaviour has always been punished.

As A. Yakovlev, a former candidate member of Politburo, has argued, the systemic persecution of persons who showed initiative and independence led to the 'mass lumpenisation' of society, which in turn spawned incompetence and irresponsibility.[5]

Within larger or traditional organisations, like (formerly) state-owned enterprises, the state bureaucracy and schools, this aversion to independent behaviour is still very much present. This attitude produced a deep-rooted lack of or fear of taking initiative.

Extreme passivity is also characteristic for many inhabitants of Zaporizhzhya, although not immediately visible. The attitude is that the world, even the immediate environment, cannot be changed. If you bring forward concrete proposals for co-operation for people in Zaporizhzhya, the first reaction is to enumerate scores of reasons why such a project is not possible. The second reaction is that the Western partner should do everything. It is an attitude of 'learned helplessness'. A deeply-rooted attitude that is very difficult to unlearn, as I have noticed.

The culture of dependence not only produces a lack of initiative, but also a lack of willingness to assume responsibility. Generally, people do not feel responsible for the tasks allotted to them. Their superiors do not credit them with competence, so there is no scope to assume responsibility. Assuming responsibility for something may have negative consequences. In

Soviet times, the people were only expected to follow orders, not to show initiative, although people found many ways to circumvent silently the orders imposed from above.

Of course, such an attitude has very negative consequences for labour ethos in general. As Hedrick Smith noticed, industriousness, discipline and efficiency did not rank high with most Soviets. According to him, one of the most notable traits in the Soviet Union was the lax national work ethic. This is not to say that people in Zaporizhzhya do not want to do a good job. However, circumstances often prevent them from doing so. Usually, in order to make sure that they work, people have to be supervised constantly.[6]

The culture of dependence and the cult of power created a general inertia in society and individual persons. One seldom finds an enthusiasm to undertake something, although with small industrial entrepreneurs I experienced quite another attitude. But they are rare in Zaporizhzhya.

Generally, Zaporizhzhya society can be described as a 'victim-society', a society in which the overwhelming majority of people feel themselves victims of their situation. The idea of shaping one's future by determined action and initiative is alien to most people. Furthermore, most people are inclined to complain about the circumstances imposed upon them, without taking any action.

The marginalisation of intellect

The fact that intelligent and competent people are often marginalised in society and economy is very conspicuous in Zaporizhzhya. Society in Zaporizhzhya seems to be the opposite of a meritocracy. Being able and intelligent is a major obstacle to obtaining positions of influence. One of the remarks I have heard from most of the inhabitants of Zaporizhzhya is that 'here they do not like clever people'. Compliance with those in power is a first requirement for position of influence. All other abilities are secondary. The result is an elite that is very incompetent. And incompetent people cannot tolerate competent people in their immediate environment. So, the specific recruitment mechanisms for influential positions in Zaporizhzhya prevent the development of competence.

Generally, and this is typical for Russian and Soviet history, the intelligentsia eschewed power. In their eyes, power is corrupt and something evil. Clever people have usually sought a career in science or arts, rather than in politics. Creative intelligence in society was not only oppressed but channelled in directions that were not threatening to those in power. Nowadays, despite the introduction of formal parliamentary democracy, nothing has changed in this respect.

Usually, positions of influence in public services, like education and health care, are distributed among the Nomenklature, i.e. decided upon by municipality or provincial administration.

With teachers, university lecturers and artists, I have noticed that discussions usually were far removed from every - day life experience. The subject of politics is avoided. Discussions may often be about the interpretation of works of art, especially literature and often have a philosophical character, but of an esoteric kind. Creative intellectual energy is channelled towards escapist themes, without any practical relevance. Hedrick Smith referred to Tatyana Tolstaya, saying that

> Russians are prone to escapism, whether it be the 'lazy, dreamy' philosophising of the intelligentsia, or the brutal, destructive and often self-destructive mass alcoholism of workers and peasants. (p. 183)

It is remarkable that among intellectuals in Zaporizhzhya there is a reluctance to write. Generally, no writing culture exists in Zaporizhzhya, or, for that matter in Ukraine and Russia at large. This is paradoxical given the rich history of literature, the central place poetry occupies in the everyday life of educated people and the huge bureaucratic paper overload.

In the West, writing letters, or writing in general, is a daily occupation for many - this is not so in Zaporizhzhya. Communication between institutions and enterprises is usually in non-written form.[7] It is normal for a director of a large state enterprise not to write letters. His secretary may have standard letters.[8] I repeatedly noticed in the academies and the universities of Zaporizhzhya that functionaries in leading positions as well as professors will write a simple letter only with great difficulties. It is not only a question of lack of experience. It is also the reluctance to put something on paper as it may be used against you.

It appeared that the head of the international department of an important academy in Zaporizhzhya, with many thousands of students, not only did not have a typewriter or a computer or a fax, but not even envelopes or stamps.

I have participated in several scientific co-operation projects with different partners in Zaporizhzhya. I always have had the problem, unlike with partners from other Central and Eastern European countries, that the Zaporizhzhya partners would often not answer my written requests. This was not related to technical difficulties but to the reluctance, as I see it, to write. It is not primarily a language problem, but, above all, a reluctance to put something on paper. According to an American colleague, witnessing the process of sending a fax to me, the rector spent many hours reformulating a simple letter to me. He originally had the impression that my Zaporizhzhya partners were involved, constantly, in an intensive exchange of letters. But they were actually busy constantly reformulating the very same fax letter.

On all levels this lack of writing culture proves to be an impediment to written forms of communication.

In writing letters, the problem is also of constructing an argument. Here, the general lack of ability to analyse as such comes to the fore, as I also noticed in the numerous interviews I had with university professors, enterprise directors and managers, politicians and functionaries.

No questions

In my interviews I always noticed a lack of ability to analyse and a lack of strategic thinking. This may be related to the fact that people were never asked to think independently, even in the universities, and also related to the fact that in the educational system they have never learnt to analyse. The educational system was geared towards the reproduction of facts rather than towards developing the ability to theorise or to analyse independently. I noticed that this is still a basic characteristic of the educational system. Universities or academies look like secondary schools in Western Europe 40 years ago. Students have an overloaded programme of classes. There are practically no seminars where texts are discussed and students have hardly any time in the curriculum for independent research or writing.

Soviet society and the Soviet educational system produced a world outlook that was very simple. The 'laws' of society and economy were laid down in the classics of Marxism-Leninism and the only question was to interpret them in the right way, which meant the interpretation of the party-state. Of course, the official world outlook and that of citizens differed but Soviet propaganda has had a profound impact on the world outlook of citizens. Also, the fact that almost everything in the individual's life was planned by the party-state, from professional career to the living place, had an enormous impact on the world outlook of citizens. Citizens had very limited scope for manoeuvre in planning their lives. Consequently they also did not learn to plan and to analyse the future in terms of alternative development paths. I have noticed in interviews that, usually, the interviewees were not able to think about the future in terms of alternative options. They lacked the ability to think in terms of hypotheses.

A peculiar phenomenon observed by Westerners lecturing in Zaporizhzhya, and elsewhere in Ukraine, is that students usually react to theories or suggestions proposed by the lecturers by asking 'is it right or wrong', or, 'is it good or bad'. Usually, students do not envisage that the world may be interpreted in different ways, or, that one particular theory may be partly adequate and partly inadequate in explaining a specific phenomenon.

This is related to the specific forms of exclusion, predominant in Soviet thinking. In political life, the adage has been 'who is not with us, is against us', instead of inclusive thinking , namely 'who is not against us, is with us'. This attitude penetrated science as well. For example, existentialist philosophy was not in line with the party-state ideology and therefore bad. This official, excluding way of looking at the world of ideas had a profound impact upon the world outlook of citizens. Related to the above described mechanisms of exclusion is the propensity to be very intolerant towards deviant opinions.[9]

The absence of reliable newsmedia furthers the inclination of people to believe gossip. Although everybody knows that Avtozaz, the local car manufacturer, used to produce very bad cars, most people believe that the car plant is the most modern in Europe. Even serious newspapers write this. The newsmedia and most citizens with whom I talked about it believe that this factory is a major asset in which foreign car makers show a lot of interest. Every time the newspapers wrote that a contract had been signed with a foreign investor (and this happened regularly), people tended to believe it, although each time the newspapers proved to be wrong.

A corollary of this simplistic world outlook is the fact that questions are seldom posed, reflecting the general lack of curiosity.

Although I am a foreigner and know about life in the West, my friends seldom asked about Western life, although few of them have ever visited the West. Generally speaking, they were not interested at all in my findings in Zaporizhzhya. They assumed, as I was regularly told, that it is impossible for a Westerner, only staying a few months in Zaporizhzhya, to write something meaningful about this town.

This is also the experience of other Westerners in Zaporizhzhya: usually there are no questions, no curiosity.[10] Partly, this is a cultural phenomenon.

It is not considered polite to pose questions. Also, people do not want to reveal a lack of knowledge.

Here we come to an important point in our observations, namely that the inhabitants of Zaporizhzhya have a peculiar attitude towards foreigners, related to the way foreigners were treated in Soviet times. Being a foreigner means being excluded from the community. At Soviet universities special courses for Soviet students taught them how to behave with regard to foreigners. There is a big divide between a foreigner and an inhabitant of Zaporizhzhya. I even experienced this with good friends. This may be related to the fact that Zaporizhzhya is still very much communist, although the party-state axis has collapsed.

It means, for example, that there is the routine reaction not to say bad things about Zaporizhzhya. For example, one of my best friends told me that beggars in Zaporizhzhya do not really need to beg and that they are usually alcoholics.

There is also the mechanical reaction not to ask foreigners questions. Foreigners who have lived for a long time in Zaporizhzhya, more than ten years, who have married Ukrainian women and are fluent in Russian, told about this persistent exclusion of foreigners. It may be an unconscious reaction. This reluctance to be open with foreigners is not only related to the patriotism that one can find everywhere in the world, but to a mechanism of exclusion that is typical for isolated communities.[11] A foreign friend, even being a friend, always remains a kind of outsider to be treated differently from one's countrymen.

Of course, this mechanism makes the analysis of the Stalinist socio-psychological syndrome by a foreigner even more difficult.

The Stalinist socio-psychological syndrome as a comprehensive mechanism

As figure A.1. shows, the constituent elements of the Stalinist socio-psychological syndrome form a interrelated whole, reinforcing each other. This is why it is so tenacious.The system described above is a system of negative feedbacks. No features are described that can be interpreted as positive. These negative feedback mechanisms can be seen as a kind of cancer in Zaporizhzhya society. Understanding of this phenomenon is crucial for grasping the essence of the present crisis of Zaporizhzhya society.

The collective programming of the minds of individuals in Zaporizhzhya has been described here.[12] It does not mean that the above description depicts adequately the average citizen of Zaporizhzhya. Such an average citizen does not exist. People in Zaporizhzhya are as diverse as they are in any other place in the world. Nevertheless, my assertion is that the overwhelming majority of inhabitants are affected by the syndrome as described above. It does not imply that most Zaporizhzhya citizens share each element of the syndrome.

Figure A.1 The Stalinist socio-psychological syndrome as a comprehensive mechanism

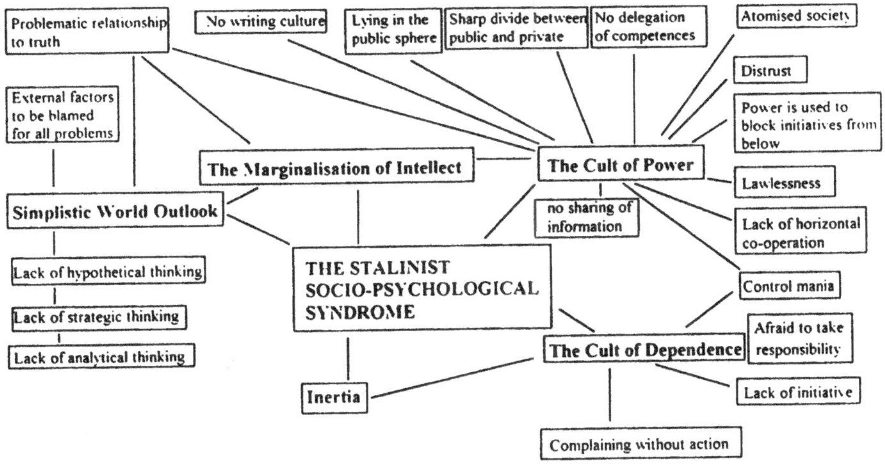

Of course, the argument around the Stalinist socio-psychological syndrome is built upon subjective impressions. However, they have been made inter-subjective as consensus arose about a draft version of the text during discussions with numerous knowledgeable people. The problem is that the hypothesis of the Stalinist socio-psychological syndrome cannot be made tangible or verified.

The properties attributed to the Stalinist socio-psychological syndrome became most pronounced in Stalin's time, although many of these properties had already developed in tsarist times and have been described in 19th century Russian literature. Six years after the independence of Ukraine and the dissolution of the Soviet empire it appears that this syndrome is very persistent and that *Homo Sovieticus* is still very much alive. [13]

Notes

1. See Etkind, Gozman, 1992. The fact that hardly any systematic analysis has been made of the Stalinist socio-psychological syndrome is related to the following factors: (1) Soviet psychology is not very well developed due to restrictions under communist rule. (2) For the few Western psychologists that are interested, in most cases the language barrier denies them access. (3) The phenomon is difficult to grasp and empirical research is difficult to envisage, which makes it unsuitable for research that is academically acceptable. As far as values are analysed in the literature dealing with cross-cultural research, it are rather the opinions of those whose attitudes are analysed, rather than deeply- rooted values. Values are analysed through the prism of opinions rather than that of behaviour (see Hofstede and Ignatow). Mental programming of people is primarily seen in their behaviour and less so in opinions about values, norms and institutions. Value surveys conducted in Russia in 1991, 1993 and 1996 showed that individual Russians reveal an adherence to moral principles comparable to that of people of most other European countries. This contrasts with the experience of many observers of Russian society. One of the researchers involved in the above mentioned surveys concluded that 'while Russian society does indeed seem to be undergoing a moral crisis, the values of individuals have remained relatively intact (Kääriänen,K.).
2. The account of Marquis de Custine in his 'Letters from Russia' (1839) shows how deeply and historically rooted is the mania for control by customs.
3. Trust is a basic value underpinning the smooth functioning of modern market economies.
4. H. Smith noticed that 'within the trusted tribal ring, the bonds are strong but outside it, the frictions are abrasive and the mistrust corrosive' (p. 182). Trust in the small circle of family and friends is relative as there is almost an absence of delicacy with respect to matters of privacy. Usually, people have not learnt to be careful with personally entrusted information.
5. Millar,Wolchik, p. 251.
6. This observation is confirmed by Dutch entrepreneurs having subsidiaries in Ukraine, who were interviewed during a seminar about Ukraine organised by the Utrecht Chamber of Commerce, December 1995.
7. Of course, all institutions were and are faced with an excessive bureaucratic paper load. But this is the filling-in of forms and not the writing of letters or other texts.
8. I have waited many hours in the secretary's office of directors of enterprises. The secretaries have typewriters while the directors have numerous telephones on their desk, the more important the director, the more telephones. However, I

seldom saw secretaries typing. They were usually calling, or talking with guests who entered the office.

9. Custine already in 1839 pointed to the deep intolerance he encountered in Russia (p. 48).
10. Custine (1839) described Russia as a nation of mutes. 'Under despotism, curiosity is synonymous with indiscretion' (p. 111).
11. I have had the same feeling when communicating to orthodox Calvinists or the inhabitants of isolated communities in the Netherlands.
12. In human mental programming, three levels can be distinguished: the individual, the collective and the universal. Mental programs are developed in the family in early childhood and reinforced in schools and organisations. It is held that these mental programmes contain a component of national culture (Hofstede, p. 11).
13. The term *'Homo Sovieticus'* is used with reluctance here as many of the characteristic behaviour patterns and values described here and usually labelled *'Homo Sovieticus'* were already visible under tsarist rule (see Custine).

Appendix 2

The Interpretation of Statistical Data in Zaporizhzhya

In Soviet times the statistical office used to be the prostitute of power. Statistical data were highly unreliable and served to hide rather than to uncover economic reality.

In general, the transition to a market economy did not mean a simultaneous improvement in the quality of statistical data. In 1994, the Economic Commission for Europe wrote that 'nowadays, the reliability of statistical data in Central and Eastern Europe is even less than under communist rule (pp. 66, 67).

The situation in Zaporizhzhya seems no exception to this rule. Peculiar in Zaporizhzhya is that all statistical material is classified and only distributed in a very small circle within the ruling elite. This prevents a debate about the quality of statistical data.

The data the statistical office gives are often contradictory and are regularly revised.

The first example of contradictory information is that about growth of industrial production.

According to the most recent figures of the statistical office (Zaporizke 1996b), in 1991 growth of industrial production was 0.4 per cent. In 1992 the decline in industrial production was 4.7 per cent, in 1993 1.2 per cent, in 1994 22.5 per cent and in 1995 10.3 per cent.

However, *Nash Gorod* (11 February 1992, p.2) gives for 1991, on the basis of data of the very same statistical office, a decline of industrial production of 1.3 per cent. In that year almost all industrial enterprises witnessed a decline, except the production of cars and recorders. In 1991, employment in industry declined by 7000 persons.

Statistical data from early 1993, as given in the report of Coopers and Lybrand (1993), give indications for an overall industrial decline in 1992 that is much more than the 4.7 per cent decline suggested by the statistical office in 1996. In the statistical bulletin for the fourth quarter of 1995, an industrial decline for 1994 of 26.4 per cent was given. Three months later, in the first bulletin of 1996, a decline of 22.5 per cent was given.

For the first nine months of 1995 industrial decline was, according to Pokhvalsky, the chairman of the province council, 10.1 per cent (*Delovaya Ukraina*, 15 November 1995, p. 1, 2). According to the statistical office, for 1995 as a whole, industrial decline was 10.3 per cent. However, six months later there was an adjustment: industrial decline was 6.1 per cent over 1995 (Zaporizke, 1996c).

All these comparisons and different data raise great doubts about the validity of the data of the statistical office.

A comparison of growth/decline of Ukrainian GDP and Ukrainian industry as given by the Ukrainian Ministry of Statistics, with industrial decline of Zaporizhzhya province as given by the Zaporizhzhya statistical office is instructive (Zaporizke 1996c).

Table A.1 Growth of GDP and industrial production in Ukraine and Zaporizhzhya province, 1991 - 1995, in percentages

	1991	1992	1993	1994	1995	cumulative
GDP Ukraine	-11.9	-17.0	+4.2	-2.5	-11.8	-49.7
Ind. production Ukraine	+4.8	-6.4	-8	-27.8	-11.5	-48.3
Ind. production Zaporizhzhya	+0.4	-4.7	-1.2	-22.5	-6.1	-28.2

Source: Zaporizhzhya Statistical Office, Ukrainian Ministry of Statistics

As the Ministry of Statistics apparently interprets the data of Zaporizhzhya Statistical Office published in the book *Ukraine in Figures for 1996*, issued by this Ministry, industrial decline in Ukraine as a whole over the period 1990 - 1996 has been 50 per cent, the recorded industrial decline for Zaporizhzhya has been 22 per cent. According to this book, Zaporizhzhya was the best- performing province amongst all Ukrainian provinces.

In Soviet times, Zaporizhzhya Statistical Office used to give better indicators for economic performance than Ukraine. According to official statistics, Zaporizhzhya per capita net material product was in 1990 23 per cent higher than the Ukrainian average (Lunina,1994).

Although there is no empirical evidence to believe that industrial decline in Zaporizhzhya has been less than for Ukraine as a whole, Zaporizhzhya Statistical Office gives the impression that Zaporizhzhya performed much better than the national average. A rough estimate by the author with respect to industrial decline in the period 1991 - 1995 for Zaporizhzhya province comes in the range of 60-70 per cent. This estimate is in line with the decline of industrial products for Ukraine as a whole as given by the Ministry of Statistics in Kiev.

Table A.2 Indicators of industrial production in Ukraine, 1990 - 1995

Type of product	Measure	1990	1995	1995/1990 (%)
electrical energy	b. kWt	295	195	66.1
iron ore	mn tons	105	50	47.6
manganese ore	1000 ton	7098	3330	46.9
cast iron	mn tons	45	19	42.2
steel	mn tons	53	23	43.4
large electrical machines	number	4708	260	5.5
electrical engines	number	11424	2035	17.8
machine tools	number	36300	6600	18.1
pressing	number	10800	1545	14.5
machine excavators	number	11162	2755	24.7
bearings	numbers	151	29	19.2
fertilizers	mn tons	4.82	2.24	46.7
sugar	1000 tons	6704	2845	42.4
textiles	mn sq m	1210	150	12.4
shoes	mn pairs	189	21	11.1
televisions	thousands	3773	250	6.6
motorcycles	thousands	103	7	6.8
bicycles	thousands	800	50	6.3

Source: Ministry of Statistics, Kyiv

Although falsification of statististical data is common practice in Ukraine, Zaporizhzhya Statistical Office seems to be one of the best falsifiers in Ukraine. A funny example is the following: according to Zaporizhzhya Statistical Office, inflation over the first half-year was 64 per cent in Zaporizhzhya, while it was over 1996 as a whole only 39.1 per cent. However, inflation in Ukraine as a whole was 80 per cent in 1996.

The second example of contradictory information is about the personnel of Avtozaz, the car manufacturer in Zaporizhzhya.

During a visit to the enterprise, our interlocutors advised that the personnel of the factory numbered 14,000 people. At the same time they gave me written, new information about the factory which stated that the number of personnel is 'about 18,000 persons'. One month later (mid-March), an employee of the factory assured me that there were only 12,000 people on the payroll of the factory, although no wages had been paid since November 1995.

According to the statistical data for the seven largest enterprises, especially prepared for the author by the Statistical Office, the personnel of Avtozaz has grown from 20,002 people in 1991 to 28,855 in 1995. The latter figure has also been given in the business plan of the enterprise.

All these figures point to confusion about the most elementary statistical data.

In the third example the Statistical Office gave us the data for the seven largest enterprises. According to the Statistical Office, the personnel of the seven largest enterprises in Zaporizhzhya increased from 90,122 in 1991 to 93,984 in 1995. These enterprises included Aluminium Enterprise, Zaporozhstal, Dnepropetsstal, Ferrosplavzavod, Transformerzavod, Avtozaz and Motor Sitch. This picture contrasts with the accounts from within the factories, Of course, here it should be noticed that there is a big difference between the formal payroll and the people that are actually paid. But even when comparing data of officially registered personnel from within the factories with the data from the statistical office, large differences appear.

According to the Statistical Office the volume of production of Transformerzavod rose in the period 1991 - 1995 by 6.5 per cent. However, the volume of production in kilowatt hours had decreased in the same period, according to data from the very same Statistical Office, by 41.5 per cent. An absurdity. And no slip of the pen!

According to the Statistical Office, the value of production of Ferrosplavzavod has increased in the period 1991 - 1995 by 122 per cent (!). The personnel of this factory has increased, according to the same Statistical Office, from 2630 to 3203 in the same period, while production declined sharply in the same period according to employees of the factory.

Therefore, the assessment of the Economic Commission for Europe probably also applies for Zaporizhzhya although the author did not have the time to make a comparison with the old statistics, produced in communist times.

How can the Statistical Office can give such absurd and contradictory information? Probably because the very few people that have access to the statistical data hardly read them, assuming that they are not very reliable. The rare individuals that study these figures probably do not have the time to analyse them or do not have the opportunity to criticise the figures. So the Statistical Office can continue to cheat those in power.

The misinformation of the Statistical Office and the secrecy around statistical data prevents authorities, scientists and journalists from adequately analysing the social and economic situation in Zaporizhzhya.

Appendix 3

The Research Process

The process of collecting information in Zaporizhzhya about Zaporizhzhya is very instructive about society and economy of Zaporizhzhya. First of all hardly anything has been written about contemporary society and economy of the town or region. This is surprising given the fact that Zaporizhzhya province has more than two million inhabitants and has experienced such dramatic changes recently. Practically all the published sources for this book are newspaper articles.

In the local newspapers most articles about enterprises were written by the directors of those enterprises. The interviews with those directors were not critical and did not touch upon sensitive issues. The account of local newspapers often contradicted the facts heard from insiders. Newspapers and weeklys published in Kiev often gave more critical accounts when writing about Zaporizhzhya. But even the quality of the best Ukrainian newspapers is quite low compared to leading newspapers in the West.

It was difficult to get hold of the most elementary information. The bulletin of Zaporizhzhya Statistical Office is considered classified material. Only 44 copies of the bulletin are distributed. Although we obtained copies of the statistical bulletins, most researchers from Zaporizhzhya have never seen this bulletin.

With the help of a junior functionary we got hold of the background reports that the firm Coopers and Lybrand made about Zaporizhzhya in 1993. In the background reports of Coopers and Lybrand there are many references to lack of information, unreliable figures and denial of access to enterprises.

The higher we climbed in the hierarchy of public authorities and enterprises, the less information we got. When a functionary made a dossier for us about environmental pollution in Zaporizhzhya, the handover of this material was prevented by his boss. Subsequently we obtained the needed material about Zaporizhzhya from the Ministry of Environment in Kyiv.

A major source of information was the interviews conducted with a large number of knowledgeable people in economy and society. However, in most cases these people appeared to be less knowledgeable than assumed. Interviewees generally could provide very little information. This may be related to unwillingness to provide information. Most probably it is also related to general lack of knowledge. The generation of knowledge about their own situation is prevented by the lack of collective learning that is related to the isolation and provinciality of Zaporizhzhya as well as the atmosphere of secrecy and unwillingness to share information.

Often, officials showed very uncivilised behaviour. For example, after several attempts we managed to make an appointment with the assistant of the chairman of the provincial council for foreign economic affairs. At the time of the meeting he did not show up. When asked, the porter informed us that he had been instructed to tell us that his boss had had to leave. Since then we never heard anything from this official.

Twice we held one day free for a visit to the steel enterprise Dneprospetsstal. Twice, on the morning of the planned visit, functionaries of the provincial administration who had organised the visit, let us know that the enterprise directors did not have time to see us.

In most cases, officials did not keep their word with respect to promises made to us. One of the authors of this book had done research in other regions of Central and Eastern Europe, but never had encountered such behaviour. These experiences are shared by Westerners living in Zaporizhzhya.

Bibliography

Anderson, P. (1978), *Passages from Antiquity to Feudalism,* London: Verso.

Baradjuk, V, Turshinov, A., Prikodko, T. (1996), 'Otshenko mashtabov tenevoj ekonomiki i ee vlijanije na dinamiku makro ekonomitsjeshkikh pokazatelej', *Ekonomika Ukraini*, November.

Bystrytsky, Y. (1995), 'The Political Philosophy of Post-Communism: Methodological Horizons in 'Political Thought', *Ukrainian Political Science Journal*, nr.1.

Coleman, D. (ed.) (1996), *Europe's Population in the 1990s,* Oxford: Oxford University Press.

Conquest, R. (1968), *The Great Terror, Stalin's Purge of the Thirties,* London: MacMillan.

Coopers.and Lybrand (1993), Strategia ekonomicheskovo razvitia Zaporozskoi oblasti Ukraini. itogovie doklad, Zaporizhzhya.

Coopers and Lybrand (1995), Privletsjennije innostrannix investitsije v zaporozsjkii region. Masterklass, 12 - 13 dekabrja, Zaporizhzhya.

Craig ZumBrunnen (1992), 'Environmental conditions', in Koropeckyj, 1992, pp. 312-359.

Crowley, S. (1992), 'Steelworkers and Mutual Dependence in the former Soviet Union', *World Politics,* 46, July.

Custine, Marquis de (1975), *Lettres de Russie.* Paris. Gallimard.

Davies, R. W. (1980), *The Socialist Offensive - The Collectivisation of Soviet Agriculture, 1929-1930,* London: MacMillan.

Dolgorudov, Y. (1995), 'Ekonomicheskoye obesnesnije strukturnoi perestroiki metallurgoi oekraini', *Ekonomika Ukraini.* October.

Dornberg, J. (1994), *Brezhnev The Mask of Power*. London: Andre Deutsch Limited.

Economic Commission for Europe (1994), *Economic Bulletin for Europe*, Vol. 46.

Echo Tchernobyl v Zaporozhye (1992), Zaporizhzhya: MP 'Bereginha'.

Egorov, I. (1996), 'Structural Changes in Russia and Ukrainian Economies: Slimming to the Third World'. Paper presented for the annual conference of the European Association for Evolutionary Political Economy, Antwerp, 7-9 November 1996.

Etkind, A., Gozmann, L. (1992), *The Psychology of Post-Totalitarianism.* London: Centre for Research into Communist Economies.

Frausum, Y. G. van; Filatotchev, I; Wright, M.; Buck. T. (1995), Privatisation and Industrial Restructuring in the Ukraine. November. Kiev: TACIS.

Greenpeace (1996), *Chernobyl: Ten Years After,* Kiev: Greenpeace Ukraine.

Gregory, P. R. (1990), *Restructuring the Soviet Economic Bureaucracy.* Cambridge: Cambridge University Press.

Hirszowicz, M. (1980), *The Bureaucractic Leviathan. A Study in the Sociology of Communism.* Oxford: M. Robertson.

Hofstede, G. (1984), *Culture's Consequences - International Differences in Work-Related Values,* London: Sage Publications.

Hirschhausen, C. von (1995), Zum Strukturwandel und der Industriepolitik in der Ukraine, Berlin, August.

Ignatow,A. (1997), 'Die mühsame Entdeckung des Individuums - Wertewandel und Wertekonflikte in Russland', *Berichte des Bundesinstituts für ostwissenschaftliche und internationale Studien*, Nr 22.

Ilyinkova, E. (1995a), *The Ukrainian Industry.* Gelsenkirchen: Institut Arbeit und Technik.

Ilyinkova, E. (1995b), *The Ukrainian Aviation Industry.* Gelsenkirchen: Institut Arbeit und Technik.

Ilyinkova, E., Kureda, N. (1995), *The Ukrainian Ferrous Metallurgy.* Gelsenkirchen: Institut Arbeit und Technik.

Johnson, S., Kaufmann, D.,Ustenko, O. (1996), 'Household Survival Strategies' in *Ukrainian Economic Review.* Vol. 11 (3).

Kääriänen, K. (1997). 'Moral Crisis or Immoral Society? Russian Values after the Collapse of Communism' *Berichte des Bundesinstituts für ostwissenschaftliche und internationale Studien*, Nr 26.

Kotkin, S. (1991), *Steeltown USSR. Soviet Society in the Gorbachev Era.*

Koropeckyi, I. S. (1992). *The Ukrainian Economy- Achievements, problems, Challenges.* Harvard: Harvard University Press.

Kubicek, P. (1996), 'Variations on Corporatist Theme: Interest Associations in Post-Soviet Ukraine and Russia', *Europe-Asia Studies.* Vol 48, Nr 1, pp. 27 - 46.

Kuzio, T.;Wilson, A. (1994), *Ukraine: Perestroika to Independence.* Macmillan.

Lukinov, I.(1995), 'Rezultati i perspektivi; rinotchnix preobrazovanie v ekonomike Ukraini', *Ekonomika Ukraini*, nr.12.

Lunina, I. (1994), 'Probleme des Regionale Finanzausgleichs in der Ukraine', *Berichte des Bundesinstituts für ostwissenschaftlich ostwissenschaftliche und internationale Studien*, Nr 11.

Lyndon Dodds, G. (1995), *A History of Sunderland.* Sunderland: Albion Press.

Malet, M. (1982), *Nestor Makhno in the Russian Civil War.* London: MacMillan Press.

Millar, J. R., Wolchik, S. (1994), *The Social Legacy of Communism.* Cambridge: Cambridge University Press.

Ministry of Statistics of Ukraine (1997), *Ukraine in Figures for 1996*, Kyiv: Naukova Dumka.

Murphy, P. (1981), *Brezhnev - Soviet Politician.* New York: McFarland & Company.

Osherki Istorii Zaporizhzhya.(1992), Zaporizhzhya: Rip 'Vidavets'.

Pirie, O. S. (1996), 'National Identity and Politics in Southern and Eastern Ukraine', *Europe-Asia Studies.* November.

Semonov,G.,Spencer Pierce.(1994), 'O strategii strukturnoi perestroiki ekonomiki promislenovo goroda', *Ekonomika Ukraini,* July.

Seton-Watson, H. (1967), *The Russian Empire 1801 - 1917.* Oxford: Oxford Press.

Sieburger,M.(1993, *Regionale Aspekte des Transformationsprozesses der Ukrainischen Wirtschaft - Die Gebiete L'wiw, Odessa und Donezk, Berichte des Bundesinstitut fur ostwissenschaftliche und internationale Studien,* nr. 38.

Smith, H. (1990), *The New Russians.* New York: Random House.

Subtelny, O. (1994), *Ukraine - A History,* Toronto: University of Toronto Press.

TACIS EDUK 9402, (1996), *Addressing the social impact of restructuring enterprises in Ukraine. Socio-economic public opinion poll,* October.

'Tenevaja ekonomika ir ganizovannaia prestupnost v ukraine: sovremenoe sostanie i problemi borbis nimi', Zerkala Nedeli, 10 February, p.5,6.

Tokarenko, I. I., Ivanov, B. J. (1994), 'Ekolokhishetkaja situatsia I zabolevajemost naselenia v Zaporozhye', *Khikiena I Sanitaria,* 1994, Nr.7.

Ukraine Municipal Utility Development and Investment Programme (1997). Volume 6, Water Supply Services Assesment. Final Report, June.

Ukraina ta ii regioni,(1995), Upravlinija z pitan ekonomiki administratsii prezidenta ukraini, spetsialnije vipusk, nr. 1, September. Kiev.

Yearbook of Labour Statistics 1996. International Labour Organisation. Geneva.

United Nations. *Demographic Yearbook.*(1995).

United Nations (1996), *Human Development Report Ukraine,* Kiev.

United Nations (1996), *Statistical Yearbook (1996).*

Zaporizke oblasne upravlinija statistiki,(1995), *Zaporizka oblast v tsifrax statistitsjnii dovidnik. 1990-1994 rik i 1 pivritsja 1995r.*

Zaporizke oblasne upravlinija statistiki,(1996a), *Pro robotu narodnovo gospodarstva zaporizkoi oblasti.*

Zaporizke oblasne upravlinija statistiki,(1996b),*Zaporizka oblast v tsifrax statistitsjnii dovidnik. 1990-1994 rik i 1995 roki.*

Zaporizke oblasne upravlinija statistiki,(1996c). *Zaporizka oblast v tsifrax, statistisjnii dovidnik. 1990-1995 rr i l. povritsjha 1996 r.*

Zaporizke oblasne upravlinija statistiki,(1997a), *Zaporizka oblast v tsifrax, statistisjnii dovidnik.* 1992, 1995,1996.

Zaporizke oblasne upravlinija statistiki (1997b), *Pro Sotshalno-ekonomitshne stanovitse Zaporizkoi oblasti za citsen 1997 roku.*

Zaporizhe oblasne upravlinija statistiki (1997c), *Zaporizka oblast v tsifrax, statistisjnii dovidnik, 1997.*

Zon, H. van.(1994), *Alternative Scenarios for Central Europe* Aldershot: Avebury.

Zon, H. van.(1995), 'Specifics of Regional Development in Central and Eastern Europe'. *Geographia Polonica,* Vol. 66, 3, November.

Zon, H. van.(1996), *The Future of Industry in Central and Eastern Europe,* Aldershot: Avebury.

Zviglyanich, V. (1996), 'The State and Economic Reform in Ukraine: Ideas, Models, Solutions'. Ukrainian *Quarterly,* Vol. LH, no 2 - 3, Summer - Fall.

Index